FISHERMAN
RESOURCES

QUESTIONS
FROM THE GOD

WHAT IS HE REALLY ASKING OF YOU?

WHO NEEDS NO
ANSWERS

CAROLYN & CRAIG WILLIFORD

SHAW BOOKS
an imprint of WATERBROOK PRESS

Questions from the God Who Needs No Answers
A SHAW BOOK
PUBLISHED BY WATERBROOK PRESS
2375 Telstar Drive, Suite 160
Colorado Springs, Colorado 80920
A division of Random House, Inc.

ISBN 13: 978-0-87788-037-0

Printed in the United States of America
2003—First edition

146502721

This book is dedicated to our favorite couples:
Robb and Tricia
and
Jay and Rachael
You bring us great joy, laughter, fellowship—and someday...grandchildren!

CONTENTS

INTRODUCTION

Questions. We need to ask them to learn about our world, to grow, and to understand more about ourselves and those around us. For an active mind, questions are essential. They're "food for the brain," so to speak, and therefore a necessity for our lives.

As toddlers we peppered our parents with dozens of questions every day as we reached out to a world that was new, exciting, and waiting to be explored. In school we discovered that asking questions was the best way to decode puzzling math problems, to grasp the complexities of English pronoun usage, and to ever begin to understand the laws of physics. As we neared adulthood we probed deeper, asking, "Who am I?" "What is truth?" and "Does God exist?" And if we were fortunate enough, we entered adulthood with a security based in God, yet still ambivalent enough about life to continue asking questions.

Almost as soon as we learned how to ask questions, we became accustomed to answering them as well. Our parents asked us anything from "Did you pick up your toys?" to "What sounds good for lunch?" And then the day came when Mom towered over us with hands on hips and demanded, "What do you think you're *doing?*" We caught on rather quickly that she wasn't looking for an explanation of our activities because she wanted to better understand what we were doing! Those questions made us realize early in life that there was indeed a different kind of query—a *rhetorical* kind—that pushed us to answer more thoughtfully and sometimes caused us to change our behavior rather than merely give an answer.

As we continued to mature, authority figures used these thought-provoking questions even more frequently. In school settings, teachers and principals called us to account for our behavior, our lateness, and our report cards, even when it was clear that they already knew the answers. Our parents asked these kinds of questions—especially throughout our teen years—to get our attention or to make a point. Even though we may have cynically thought the answers were obvious, adults constantly asked us rhetorical questions to make us evaluate, think, and take responsibility for our behavior. And, if we become parents as adults, we often find ourselves doing the very thing we vowed we'd never do: asking our kids the same kinds of questions!

Have you noticed that God asks questions too? He first questioned Adam and Eve in the Garden of Eden, then he confronted the patriarchs, and later, throughout the history of Israel, he probed the hearts and minds of judges, prophets, and kings. In the New Testament we find that Jesus continued this practice by using questions as an incredible teaching tool: With deep scrutiny, he drew men and women to himself, often using story and parable to frame his insightful and searching questions. More than any others, the questions God poses cause us to step back, reflect, and deeply examine ourselves. Insightful and intrusive, these questions stab straight into the soul. They simply cannot be ignored.

In rare situations throughout Scripture and in the midst of extraordinary circumstances, God asked people concise, direct questions in *rhetorical* form. Can you imagine being in Adam's place, having just knowingly disobeyed your Creator, when God inquired, "Where are you?" Or would you have wanted to be in Jonah's shoes when God confronted him, asking, "Have you any right to be angry?" The dictionary defines this unusual construction as "a question to which no answer is expected or one for which only one answer may be made." But the dictionary writers weren't referring to God when they composed that definition! For when God asks us a rhetorical question, he does indeed expect an answer. His questions, in fact, *demand* answers, but they're for our benefit, not his. God needs no answers to his questions, and he doesn't ask them in order to obtain information or discover something he doesn't already know. The fact is, an omniscient God has no need to ask questions, period, not ever. Yet he does ask questions to help us look beyond the surface of things and think more deeply about life. For example, when God asked Jacob, "What is your name?" the reader certainly understands that God had an agenda that went beyond a mere name—and that Jacob had best pick up on that agenda too!

But do God's probings apply only to whom they were first addressed? We, too, can mine an incredible wealth from these questions; their timeless themes and jarring directness command our attention even today. While skimming or reading through a Scripture passage, we may become complacent and miss the significance of what God is saying. But when he interjects himself into the affairs of men and women, stabbing through time with an inquiry such as "Will not the judge of the earth do right?" we simply cannot skim over that. Suddenly we're compelled to interact with a God who desires to meet with his people. We must take in the full meaning of what he has asked, look deeply within ourselves, and *answer*— in our *own* words—*to our God.*

This study will explore the profound questions God asked throughout the Old Testament, queries that draw our interest and ultimately compel us to ask questions too. God's rhetorical questions are incredible opportunities. He does not need our answers, but he asks because, out of his unfathomable love, he desires intimacy with his creation. He has already asked the questions that comprise the richest substance of life. Do we have the courage to look within ourselves and answer him?

"WHERE ARE YOU?"

GENESIS 3:1-19

And they hid from the LORD God among the trees of the
garden. But the LORD God called to the man, "Where are you?"
—GENESIS 3:8-9

The unspeakable had just happened: Eve succumbed to the serpent's lies, ate the forbidden fruit, and gave some to Adam. The results of Adam and Eve's sin were instantly evident: Their "eyes...were opened, and they realized they were naked" (verse 7). Before they sinned, Adam and Eve enjoyed a union of incredible vulnerability and intimacy; afterward, they attempted to "hide" from each other. Before, they knew only security and acceptance in each other's presence, but afterward, they felt exposed—physically, emotionally, psychologically. Compare this experience with Genesis 2:25: "The man and his wife were both naked, and *they felt no shame*" (emphasis added). A catastrophic break in their relationship had occurred—and they had built the first wall between them.

But the irreparable damage to Adam and Eve's relationship was only the beginning of the ramifications of their sin. When God first placed man in the garden, he and Adam communicated frequently in a close and loving relationship. In his interactions with Adam, God told Adam what he could and could not eat, he expressed interest in Adam's naming of the animals, and he was concerned that Adam was alone and in need of a suitable helper. These interactions indicate an ease of conversation and comfortable companionship that suggest intimacy in their relationship. Even more significant, as verses 8-10 indicate, God regularly—perhaps daily—came to walk "in the garden in the cool of the day," where Adam and Eve joined him for fellowship. But the moment they sinned, the intimacy, the familiarity, and the communication were shattered. For God found their meeting place *empty*. Once again, Adam and Eve's sin had sent them into hiding.

BREAKING GROUND

As a child, apart from playing hide-and-seek, did you ever hide somewhere or from someone or did you ever want to hide? What kind of situation caused you to feel a need to do this?

Were you successful in your efforts to hide? Why or why not?

Read Genesis 3:1-19.

THE DECEIVER'S QUESTION

Before they fell into sin, Adam and Eve fellowshiped with their God in complete and total openness. In their nakedness—and, at that point, sinlessness—before the Creator, the couple never experienced the atmosphere of risk, the isolation of walls, any feelings of vulnerability, or the ache of insecurity. Adam and Eve hid nothing from God because there was nothing to hide!

But then the Deceiver—Satan—posing as a snake, came to Eve and revealed his true nature as a liar. Setting the stage by enticing Eve into a web of her own lies concerning God's instructions about the Tree of the Knowledge of Good and Evil, Satan blatantly twisted God's directive ("You will not surely die," verse 4), questioned God's character, and skillfully tempted Eve with the benefits of disobeying the Creator's commands ("God knows that when you eat...you will be like God," verse 5). The Tempter is indeed skilled at twisting and distorting God's will for us.

At that point, the damage was done. The rending between God and man would result in dire consequences. In their shame and misery, Adam and Eve sought out their own futile remedy for their transgression: fig leaves, sewn together with hands stained by sin. But that pitiful attempt to repair the damage didn't go unnoticed, and God confronted them. Their response? Adam blamed the woman—and ultimately God—when he declared that she was "the woman *you* put here with me" (verse 12, emphasis added). Eve then passed the blame to Satan.

But there were no acceptable excuses, alibis, or explanations. And fig leaves would not prove adequate for the enormity of their sin. Instead, sin demanded judgment and resulted in painful consequences, and the only way to atone for it was through blood sacrifice. As one consequence for their sin, God pronounced that Adam and Eve were no longer privileged to live in the garden, and he drove them out. But even as they felt the deep pain of leaving the garden, God still showed them mercy and grace. Lovingly clothing them in garments of animal skin, God granted them a temporary covering for their sin through the sacrifice of animals. Only later would true and complete atonement come through Christ's blood sacrifice, when he would "crush [the serpent's] head" (verse 15).

First Looks

1. The Scripture text proves God's love for his creation, even though Adam and Eve willfully sinned. Where and how is this shown? Give specifics.

2. Based on verses 14-19, make a list of what was cursed and what was not. What important implications might this pronouncement have had for Adam and Eve?

THE QUESTION IN AN EMPTY GARDEN

God is complete in himself, so he cannot truly feel lonely. But can you hear the cry of aloneness he must have uttered in this now-empty garden? He had come to the garden already aware of what Adam and Eve had done; he was indeed all knowing, and Adam's absence, therefore, was not and never could be a surprise to him. Still, the question God cried out into the silent and empty garden pathway—their pathway—hauntingly echoed his pain for the once intimate relationship now broken. Gone.

Where are you?

God had come, seeking fellowship with Adam and Eve. But they were not there. Are you, like us, amazed and awed that God seeks intimate fellowship with his creation? He has no needs, period. He did not need a creation to worship him, but still he created. He did not require intimate communion with his creation, yet he sought it. And when he came to the garden, he was still seeking fellowship with Adam and Eve, even though he was fully aware of their sin.

It is important to note the vast difference between the question God did ask and the one he could have asked, one that we probably would have expected: "Why are you hiding?" God, as the Righteous Judge, would demand an accounting with this question. He would insist upon an answer and would have every right to do so. But instead, the question our loving God asked rings with desire—a desire for his creation to answer the query, to come back to him, to know his continued longing for intimacy. In God's choice of words for this significant question, we see a foreshadowing of his plan for ultimate reconciliation with the human race through the death of his Son.

Adam must have expected God to ask, "Why are you hiding?" because that is the question he answered. Had he already rehearsed his reply to that question? And does this explain why he ignored the actual query God posed? Certainly, Adam never expected God to reach out to him with tenderness. Adam, probably shocked and shamed by God's reaction and question, pathetically responded as we still do today: with excuses, rationalizations, blame. Judgment was swift to come, but so was a shadow of the cross in the sacrifice of animals for coverings.

Where are you?

Certainly, no one can read these words without realizing that this God is not at all an impersonal force who stands back from his creation and watches dispassionately or cruelly. Inherent in God's sorrowful cry is a longing for intimate fellowship with his creation, a longing that defies explanation or logic. That longing could only be the result of one thing: love.

TAKING IT IN

3. Describe how Adam and Eve shirked responsibility for their sin by resorting to blame. In what blatant as well as subtle ways did they blame each other and God?

4. What do you think is the significance of God's asking the question, "Where are you?" as opposed to "Why are you hiding?" Which question appears to offer more hope to Adam and Eve? Why?

5. What can we infer from Adam's response in verses 10-12? Do you think Adam was caught off guard by God's question? How do you know? What evidence suggests that he was (or was not) defensive?

THE QUESTION THAT MOVES BEYOND THE GARDEN

God's rhetorical query wasn't only for Adam and Eve; it is a question for the ages, a question for you, for us. When God enters that place where he would commune with you...when he desires intimacy with you, his child...when he finds that you are not where you should be...he still asks, "Where are you?" And, like Adam and Eve, we are called to answer his question!

But we can answer only by focusing on God. Where we are is determined by him alone—not by our perspective, by the spirituality of others, or by our feelings, guesses, or intuition. God is the beginning and center of determining who and what and where we are. His Word sets the guidelines for our "garden," and prayer leads us toward the specific "pathway" he has called us to walk with him.

From the Scripture text, it's clear that Adam and Eve had enjoyed a regular, intimate relationship and time of communication with their Creator. We glean a sense of the closeness they shared: They regularly enjoyed mutual fellowship and conversation as they walked together in the cool of the day. From this short, precise description, we understand that Adam and Eve had been "experiencing relationship" rather than "practicing religion." But we also see that there is a vast difference between the genuine connectedness they had with God before they sinned and the actions they now took out of a sense of duty or guilt. Are you seeking intimate relationship with God? Or are you simply "performing" the disciplines that define spirituality?

We also have much to learn from Adam and Eve's sinful reactions: When God confronted Adam and Eve with their sin, they placed blame elsewhere, refused to accept responsibility, and essentially denied the reality of their sin. Certainly, we all have this natural tendency; it's a temptation we constantly face. Denial is an incredibly strong and destructive force. When we deny reality in our lives, we hinder God's Spirit from pointing out our sin and leading us to repentance and change.

Though Adam and Eve attempted to deny their sin, God continually drew them back to the reality that was right in front of them: Sins we are blind to are still there, whether or not we admit their existence! It takes great humility and courage to accept responsibility for our sin, fully and unequivocally, but it is only from this position that we can fully embrace God's offer of tender forgiveness and unconditional love.

MAKING IT REAL

Throughout this section, try to concentrate completely on God's perspective on this question: Where am I in my relationship with God? (Avoid focusing on feelings, guesses, intuition, an erroneous personal perspective, or on comparisons to the spirituality of others.)

Where Are You in the Intimacy of Your Communication with God?

6. Do you have a regular time and place set aside to talk with God? Why are you meeting him there? What is motivating you?

Do you meet with him out of pure enjoyment of your relationship—or out of guilt?

Where Are You in Your Willingness to Accept the Reality of Sin in Your Life?

7. In what areas of your life, if any, are you blaming others or your circumstances for your problems rather than assuming full responsibility for them?

Where Are You? Naked and Not Ashamed—Or Exposed and Afraid?

8. In verse 8, when Adam and Eve knew their shame, they hid from the One who loved them most. What incredible irony! The very Source of love and forgiveness—the only One who had the ability to heal them in every way—was the One they avoided. In what ways do you tend to hide from God? In what ways, if any, are you hiding from him now? Why are you hiding from him? To help you be honest, think of issues you avoid

working on. What frightens you? What makes you feel insecure? Ask God to reveal to you any areas of your life that you might be in denial about.

Where Are You in Relation to Your Ability to Take Risks and Be Vulnerable?

9. To grow in intimacy, we must be vulnerable with one another and, especially, with our God. Are you able to be vulnerable with God? What exactly does that look like in your life?

10. With whom are you vulnerable? How is that different from your vulnerability with God? Does one kind of vulnerability teach, feed, and fuel the other? Explain.

Where Are You in Your Trust in God's Love Toward You?

11. Evidently, Adam and Eve assumed that God would be shocked
by their sin and would pull away from them if they openly and
immediately confessed what they had done. Consequences
obviously did come, but amazingly God still pursued a relationship with them. Are you holding some of your sin back from
God, assuming that he will be shocked by what you've done or
thought? What does that say about your trust in God and his
love for you? What is your trust or lack of trust based upon?

"Is Anything Too Hard for the Lord?"

Genesis 18:1-15

*Then the LORD said to Abraham, "Why did Sarah laugh
and say, 'Will I really have a child, now that I am old?'
Is anything too hard for the LORD?"*

—Genesis 18:13-14

God keeps his promises. Even in times of tremendous uncertainty throughout the world, we can know this beyond a doubt. Though we may face fears of serious health problems and death, we can cling to that truth. And no matter what insecurities we experience during major transitions in our lives, we can count on the unchanging One. The theme God teaches and reinforces time and again through his interaction with his people Israel is this: He is a promise keeper!

Yet too often when we attempt to apply this truth in our lives by demonstrating an unwavering faith in God, we falter. If we really do believe that he keeps his promises, why do we find it so hard to trust him when our child rebels? when our spouse is seriously ill? when we're waiting for answers concerning a job interview and a possible relocation? when we face yet another month of infertility? If your faith seems to waver at times, take heart and be encouraged because you're not alone! Thousands of years ago those great pillars of the faith, Abraham and Sarah, experienced similar doubts concerning God's ability to keep his promises.

When God first called Abram to become "a great nation" (Genesis 12:2), he and Sarai were still young enough to have children. (Abram and Sarai were their original names.) Believing his God and demonstrating faithful obedience, Abram packed up all of his belongings and, along with his entourage, traveled to the land that God promised would one day belong "to [Abram's] offspring" (Genesis 12:7). But years went by as Abram and Sarai waited for the promise to be fulfilled. In the meantime God intervened and saved Sarai from the consequences of Abram's deceptive lies to Pharaoh. Later, Abram rescued his wayward nephew, Lot, from captivity. Throughout these many years, to Abram and Sarai's bewilderment, Sarai remained barren. (We wonder if they asked, "Why, God?")

Finally, God must have infused Abram and Sarai with renewed hope when he initiated a covenant with them: A "smoking firepot with a blazing torch" (Genesis 15:17) passed between the sacrificed carcasses, symbolizing that God intended to keep his promises. But then even more years passed, and Sarai still did not conceive. So she gave her Egyptian maidservant, Hagar, to Abram as his wife, hoping that Hagar would bear him a child before he died. And soon, Hagar gave birth to a son. This irony must have caused Sarai incredible agony.

Eventually, God established the covenant of circumcision with Abram and changed his servants' names: Abram was given the name *Abraham*, and Sarai became *Sarah*. Yet Sarah remained childless. By the time God once again reassured Abraham of the promise—"But my covenant I will establish with Isaac, whom Sarah will bear to you by this time next year." (Genesis 17:21)—Sarah was old, well past childbearing age.

That background sets the stage for a visit from three amazing men to

Abraham and Sarah. What have Abraham and Sarah faced? Promises not yet come true. Barrenness. And very little hope. What message could these men bring to this disheartened couple?

BREAKING GROUND

Can you remember a time when you had high hopes for something only to see those hopes dashed? Briefly describe that time and how you responded.

How did you respond the next time you felt hope rise in your heart? Were you able to continue hoping or did you guard those hopes because of past disappointments? Explain.

Read Genesis 18:1-15.

WHEN THE KNOCK AT THE DOOR IS UNEXPECTED COMPANY

When God wanted to make an announcement of great significance to people during Old Testament times, he often sent an angel—or even Christ himself in preincarnate form.[1] For this important interaction with Abraham and Sarah, he sent Christ and two angels. Can you imagine what an imposing trio these three must have been? Without warning they suddenly appeared "near the great trees of Mamre" (verse 1), close to Abraham and Sarah's tent. No wonder Abraham apparently jumped up from his afternoon rest and rushed out to greet them with a humble bow.

Abraham then hastened to meet their every need. The Scripture text points out that he *hurried* to Sarah and asked her to bake bread; then he *ran* to select a calf, which he gave to a servant, who *hurried* to prepare it. We can surmise that Abraham recognized immediately that these were no ordinary guests. And if he understood that they were heavenly visitors, perhaps he also anticipated receiving some sort of blessing, prophetic announcement, or offer of help. We can only guess.

Possibly sensing the magnitude of this visit, Abraham also went to great lengths to show them the utmost respect and hospitality. He "bowed low to the ground" (verse 2) when he first greeted them. He referred to Christ as "my Lord" (verse 3) and twice referred to himself as "your servant" (verses 3,5). After he had served his guests their meal, he stood by, watching and waiting, evidently eager to provide for any further needs.

---

1. Many scholars believe that the Angel of the Lord, who appeared to people throughout the Old Testament (as we'll see in other chapters in this book), was actually Christ in preincarnate form. Others see these "messengers" as beings who are distinct from God. Since there is no definitive scriptural proof for either view, we have elected to interpret these angelic visitations as the preincarnate appearances of Christ himself.

And what about Sarah? What was she doing while these special guests conversed with her husband? She gave in to a weakness we all can admit to: eavesdropping! As Sarah listened at the entrance to the tent, she "laughed to herself" (verse 12) when the Lord pronounced that "about this time next year...Sarah...will have a son" (verse 10). But God wasn't about to let Sarah off the hook so easily. He wasn't going to let her continue to hide—not from him, nor from her own reaction. Once again his probing question prompted a response we've seen before: Sarah ignored his query and responded with fear, denial, and a lie.

FIRST LOOKS

1. What specific detail did God give Abraham in verse 10 about his (God's) part in the long-awaited birth of Isaac?

2. Abraham's homage and hurried hosting point to the fact that he immediately recognized these men as heavenly guests. What does that reveal about where Abraham was both spiritually and morally?

3. Rather than appearing as the burning bush, a blazing torch, or a smoking firepot, God chose to appear to Abraham as a hungry

man. Why is it significant that God fellowshiped with Abraham this way?

4. What difference is there between laughing to oneself and laughing out loud? Why do you think Sarah lied about laughing? What would have been a completely truthful answer?

EXPECTATIONS, PROMISES, PERCEPTIONS, AND TRUTH

We would probably all agree that Abraham and Sarah had been on a long and trying journey with the Lord. When God first met with Abraham those many years before, the father of Israel was younger and more trusting, leaving behind all that was familiar merely because God asked him to "go to the land I will show you" (Genesis 12:1). But by the time the three heavenly visitors came, Abraham and Sarah were old, "well advanced in years" (Genesis 18:11), and no longer naively trusting. They were not the same people they once were.

Sarah's laughter, at first appearance, calls us to judge her as shallow. Why couldn't she simply trust in God's ability to keep his word? Instead, she *laughed* in response to the Lord's reference to her imminent pregnancy and the birth of a son! And although she laughed to herself rather than out loud, the meaning was the same: She doubted God's promise—and his ability to keep that promise. And in doubting God's promise to her and her husband, she also doubted his promise to all who would come after them—the offspring who would become a "great nation" (Genesis 12:2).

But before we judge Sarah too harshly, let's examine the reason she questioned her ability to still bear a child, a reason we all have probably struggled with at some point in our lives. Sarah's faith faltered because it was based solely upon physical evidence. She yielded to illusionary perceptions because she expected God to operate only within the bounds and laws of the physical realm. Since her body was well past childbearing age, she assumed that she would never be able to get pregnant, let alone give birth. And she believed that God was also limited by the same physical world she perceived. Because she judged that God had waited too long, she believed he would never be able to fulfill his promise.

But Sarah should have been looking at the world from God's perspective. Our great God is never limited by the physical world, and he appears to take great delight in working outside the narrow confines of our expectations and perceptions. Old in years? What is that to a God who is beyond the limitations of time and space, whose Spirit exists in all time, simultaneously? A womb that can no longer bear a child? How could that possibly keep God—the creator of life itself—from miraculously causing that womb to spring to life once again? Sarah should have joined God in delighted rather than cynical laughter, as he totally disregarded her limited expectations, narrow perceptions, and the confines of her physical world.

God was actively advancing his plan for blessing Israel—and eventually all humankind—through Abraham and Sarah's descendents. Demonstrations of his power, majesty, and trustworthiness were all inherent and intentional parts of his plan to fulfill that promise to his people!

TAKING IT IN

5. What's the difference between what we sometimes *expect* and what God *promises?* Do they sometimes overlap? When we confuse the two, how might that affect our trust and faith in God?

6. It appears that God purposefully waited until Sarah was past childbearing age to fulfill his promise. What purpose do you think he might have had for doing so? How would that delay have benefited Abraham and Sarah?

7. What promises has God made to those of us who are his children? List some of these promises, including Scripture

references. Make sure that all the promises you list are true rather than unrealistic expectations on your part about what you think God has promised you.

THE QUESTION MEANT TO SILENCE A LAUGH

Once again, a direct question from God reverberates through the ages, crossing time, cultures, and experience. The query, "Is anything too hard for the LORD?" calls us to stop, reflect, and evaluate how we view our God. Do we really perceive and accept him as a God of truth, One who is faithful, trustworthy, and powerful?

Superficial and pat answers do not reach to the heart of this issue. We have to probe deeply, asking ourselves questions that will reveal any differences between our spoken beliefs and our true, heartfelt beliefs. It's easy to boldly announce that God is faithful, trustworthy, and powerful, but do we operate that way? Do our actions match our beliefs? Do our day-to-day lives reveal a practicing trust in God?

To discover the areas where we—like Sarah—doubt God's character, we'll need to uncover the true objects of our trust. Since we've probably been less than truthful in the past—possibly lying to God and to ourselves—we may need to begin by admitting our self-deception. Next, we'll need to examine key events in our lives, the times when we were worried and attempted to manipulate people and events in an effort to feel more secure. What were we trusting in at those times? God? Ourselves or other people (their abilities or our own)? Things (bank accounts, jobs, homes)?

Finally, we must ask ourselves, Am I viewing my life from God's viewpoint or from my own limited and sinful perspective? The irony is that when we accept a narrow, human worldview, we limit God's power in our lives. Instead, we must open our hearts and minds to his often unfathomable guidance and wisdom: He may have a plan for us that is beyond what we could ever begin to imagine.

As for Sarah, being pregnant and giving birth in her old age were totally beyond her comprehension. But a mere nine months later, her perspective had been miraculously expanded by a great, good, and gracious God to include the tiny, precious face of her son, Isaac. *Is anything too hard for the LORD?* When viewed through God's definition of *hard,* we think not.

MAKING IT REAL

8. When was the last time you awoke in the night, worrying about something? What were you worrying about? Since you evidently weren't able to trust God and rest in him, what was the actual object of your trust? You may want to list all the key times in your life when you were intensely worried. Through prayer, discern the actual object of your trust during each of those times. What can you do to change these patterns so that you will place your trust in God in the future?

9. Sometimes our expectations put limits around a promise. In Sarah's case, she limited God's promise by expecting that she could only give birth to a son if she were of childbearing age. When, if ever, have you put limits around one of God's promises to you? In what ways were you also limiting God's power?

10. Though Abraham and Sarah were evidently expecting something from their guests, we can glean from Sarah's reactions that she obviously was *not* anticipating the magnitude of her guest's announcement. Describe a time, if any, when you were hoping for a specific answer and were surprised to receive something far beyond your expectations. Has God ever answered your prayers in a way that was not what you asked but was much better? Explain.

11. List some of your hopes and dreams. But here's the challenge: How do you keep your hopes and dreams from becoming expectations? When exactly *does* a hope become an expectation?

THREE

"WHAT IS YOUR NAME?"

GENESIS 32:1-32

Jacob replied, "I will not let you go unless you bless me."
The man asked him, "What is your name?"
"Jacob," he answered.

—GENESIS 32:26-27

Unfortunately, North Americans don't practice the creative traditions for naming children that other cultures do. In some countries—in certain parts of India, for example—many parents wait until the child has reached an age when he or she demonstrates a unique personality; at that time they replace a temporary name with a permanent one that better reflects the child's inner character. (You may be thinking that our traditions are much safer, since your new name might very well be something you wouldn't particularly want to advertise to the world!)

Naming children does have some import in North American culture, too: Many parents take into account family heritage, ancestors' names, birth order, and their family's country of origin, for instance. Often, the *meaning* of a name is of particular consequence. For example, when we chose the name *Joshua* for our second son, we did so because the biblical

Joshua was a man of great integrity and courage; we also loved that it comes from the word *Savior* and literally means "Yahweh saves." Names of great significance can put pressure on a child to succeed or can challenge him or her to achieve great things for God. Either way, the child certainly understands that he or she was named with a purpose in mind.

As the firstborn twin of Rebekah, Esau received a name that was carefully chosen. He was described as being "red" and "hairy" (Genesis 25:25), so the wordplay for his name included links to *Edom* (which is related to the word for "red") and *Seir*, which is similar to the word *hairy*. Maybe more important, Edom would one day have a great impact on the Israelites, for that's the area where Esau later settled. The Edomites were to become fierce warriors who would plague the Israelites.

Jacob's name was also full of symbolism: When he emerged from his mother's womb, he was grasping his brother Esau's heel. Jacob was so named because the word means "he grasps the heel" or, figuratively, "he deceives." And Jacob would indeed live up to that foreboding name many times throughout his life!

Breaking Ground

Do your first and middle names have special significance? Explain. Were you named after someone? Why?

If you could choose a new name that best describes who you are today—your inner character—what name would that be? Why do you think that name fits you?

Read Genesis 32:1-32.

A Rose by Any Other Name

By the time we catch up with Jacob in Genesis 32, he had already caused two major conflicts. Now he was on his way to yet another potentially violent encounter. When he had last seen his twin brother, Jacob (with his mother's help) had tricked his father, Isaac, into giving him the blessing that, according to tradition, was intended for the firstborn son. Needless to say, Esau was not happy with this turn of events and even threatened to kill his conniving brother. Rebekah rightfully feared for Jacob's life, so she finagled a way for Isaac to send Jacob away to Paddan Aram, where her father, Laban, lived.

But Jacob soon found that trouble followed him to Paddan Aram. He fell in love with Laban's daughter Rachel and readily agreed to work seven years for her hand in marriage. (Now that's a picture of being smitten!) But this time the deceiver himself was fooled, for on the morning after the wedding, Jacob discovered that his veiled bride was really Leah, Rachel's sister. Laban boldly announced, "It is not our custom here to give the younger daughter in marriage before the older one" (Genesis 29:26). So Jacob was allowed to marry Rachel only after he had married Leah—for seven more years of work! (Jacob was given Rachel *before* he worked the seven years [see 29:27].)

Still the one to scheme and plan, Jacob now turned his efforts toward increasing his wealth by amassing more livestock. It wasn't long before he accomplished just that through a combination of trickery and God's blessing. Since his sheep came from his father-in-law's flocks, Laban's "attitude toward [Jacob] was not what it had been" (Genesis 31:2). No longer welcome in Paddan Aram, Jacob was instructed by God to "Go back to the land of your fathers" (31:3).

But even Jacob's journey to his homeland was not without problems. After Jacob secretly fled Paddan Aram with his family and possessions, Laban came charging after him. Rachel had stolen some of her father's household idols, and she continued to hide them while Laban searched all of Jacob's tents. Fortunately, however, Laban and Jacob agreed to make a covenant, and they parted in peace. (But unfortunately, Rachel kept those idols.)

Then, as Jacob continued on his way home, God graciously and miraculously reminded Jacob that he was with him. Just as Jacob met angels on his journey to Paddan Aram (immortalized in the song "Jacob's Ladder"), once again God sent angels to meet him as he was about to cross over into Esau's territory (see Genesis 32:1).

With that reassuring reminder, Jacob was now able to concentrate fully on the potentially dangerous task before him: confronting his brother, Esau. Sending word ahead of his arrival, Jacob referred to Esau as "my master" and called himself "your servant Jacob" (verse 4). Then he closed, saying, "Now I am sending this message to my lord, that I may find favor in your eyes" (verse 5).

After receiving a vague and cryptic response from messengers—"Esau...is coming to meet you, and four hundred men are with him" (verse 6)—Jacob began to panic. He divided his family and possessions into two groups and cried out to his God for help and protection. Then he chose hundreds of animals as gifts for Esau, and after sending his wives, maidservants, children, and possessions safely across the stream of Jabbok, Jacob was left alone. The stage was set for an amazing confrontation. This time there would be no scheming, no conniving, no devious planning. Jacob was about to meet a Man who would change him forever.

First Looks

1. What did Jacob do to attempt to control the meeting with Esau? What plans did he carry out? What appeared to backfire on him?

2. What was significant about God's sending angels to Jacob when he left the land of his fathers and then again right before he returned? What messages might God have been giving to him?

3. Jacob named the place where the angels appeared *Mahanaim*, exclaiming, "This is the camp of God!" (verse 2). Since Mahanaim means "two camps," to what other camp besides

the one in Mahanaim could Jacob have been referring? What two camps would meet in his imminent future? What other camps were significant in Jacob's life?

4. It's fascinating to watch the interplay between the two brothers in the opening verses of chapter 32. List some examples of their maneuvers or attempts to control each other. Do you think both were responding out of fear? What evidences in the text appear to prove or disprove this?

Read Genesis 32:22-28 again.

WHAT'S IN A NAME?

In verse 22 we read that "Jacob got up and took his two wives, his two maidservants and his eleven sons and crossed the ford of the Jabbok." Since we're specifically told he got up during the night, we can assume that he had probably been sleeping. Could he possibly have awakened sometime earlier, tossing and turning with worry? We can only speculate about that, but it is apparent that he got up to *do* something. Jacob sent his most precious possessions across the stream—immediately. We can only surmise that he planned to follow right away—was he doing a last-minute check to see that all were accounted for?—but if so, that plan was not to be. For once Jacob was alone, he was accosted, but not by a verbal confrontation or a mortal man. Instead, Jacob was challenged to *physically* wrestle this *immortal* Man—for the remainder of the night until dawn!

Throughout this nightlong struggle, Jacob had no idea who his Assailant was. How typical of Jacob the deceiver to wrestle with another, never submitting even though his Adversary was unknown. Jacob had already contended with Esau and Laban. With this Foe, however, he appeared to have met his match: This Man eventually forced Jacob to surrender by using supernatural means. When he touched the socket of Jacob's hip, forever shriveling the tendon, Jacob was crippled. But even though he was defeated, Jacob still stubbornly refused to let the Man go.

That moment of Jacob's disabling must have been incredible. Instant, supernatural, and decisive, this action caused Jacob to recognize that his Opponent was none other than God himself. (This Man was Jesus Christ, "God in flesh.")[2] Fearing for his very life now that he had taken in the significance of what was happening, Jacob made a quick decision: He clung to the Man, pleading for a blessing. This was a critical moment between the two wrestlers, for God then asked Jacob a question filled with layers of meaning: "What is your name?" (verse 27). Deceptively simple, easily answered. Unless your name was Jacob. The *deceiver*.

Suddenly, Jacob was forced to admit his true character: his deceptions, lies, and schemes. Face to face with a righteous God, he had no choice but to take full responsibility for all of his past sins. Was there a flash of

---

2. See note on page 20 for information regarding the preincarnate Christ.

embarrassment in his answer? Did he possibly stutter just a moment, choking over the word *Jacob?* Was he ashamed to admit that he had lived up to the symbolism of his name?

In that moment, Jacob must have recognized the utter futility of his struggle. In the past he had successfully schemed against and battled with his foes, depending upon his wits and natural physical abilities to accomplish his goals. (See Genesis 27:18-29 and 30:31-43, for example.) But this time Jacob had wrestled literally all night and still could not win the battle. He realized that he could fight his hardest and yet never defeat this Assailant. Could it be that Jacob grasped that it was useless to strive against the very One who created him? Maybe he finally accepted that it was time to put aside his scheming and struggling and *allow God to fight for him.*

But God still had more to teach Jacob, and the next lesson would have everlasting consequences for him, for the nation of Israel, and for us. By renaming Jacob *Israel,* God decisively called his stubborn, contentious patriarch to deep change. No longer "the deceiver," Israel was now "one who struggles with God" or "God fights." This new name would be a constant reminder to Jacob and the nation of Israel (which would come through his twelve sons) that *God would fight for them.* God promised Abraham, Isaac, and Jacob that from their lineage would come a great nation. Neither threats from enemies nor a woman's barrenness nor angry brothers would ever be able to hinder God. Above all, God would keep his promises.

Taking It In

5. Apparently firmly believing in his own strength and ability to overcome, Jacob fought doggedly until the Man crippled him. What impact did this have on Jacob's ambition and need for

dominance, control, and success? Why do you think the Man ended the struggle the way he did?

6. Why do you think Jacob clung to the Man, begging for a blessing? At that moment he must have been aware that he was completely at this Being's mercy and could offer him nothing. What would be accomplished by Jacob's request for a blessing?

7. The last time Jacob asked for a blessing, his father, Isaac, had asked for Jacob's name. At that time Jacob lied to his father to steal the blessing from Esau. What significance do you find in the repetition of that question this time? What could the symbolism mean for Jacob?

Read Genesis 32:29-32 again.

WHY DO YOU ASK MY NAME?

At this point, Jacob turned the tables. He asked the Man, "Please tell me *your* name" (verse 29, emphasis added). We don't know why he asked this question, but God called Jacob to self-evaluation by responding, "Why do you ask my name?" (verse 29). Once again, God pushed one of his children to examine his heart motives. His point was to make Jacob—now Israel—ponder *why* he was asking this question. Was Jacob seeking more assurance that this was indeed the Lord? Was he somehow still scheming? Whatever the reason, it's noteworthy that the Lord did not answer but instead responded with a question.

Ironically, it was not until this moment that God blessed Jacob. We can only imagine what silent messages were exchanged between the two of them as they wrestled—the looks they traded, the tightening or loosening of Jacob's hold upon the Lord, how Jacob's painful hip affected his ability to respond. And we have no recorded words for that blessing—what God said, how it was done. But certainly God spoke to Jacob's heart as he blessed him, granting him a measure of peace. That calm and peace became evident through yet another naming: Jacob called this place *Peniel,* which means "face of God." Having miraculously survived this face-to-face encounter with God, Jacob commemorated the occasion by using a phrase that normally elicited fear—the Israelites believed that seeing God's face brought instant death—but in this case brought praise.

The significance of a face-to-face encounter with God had deep meaning for Jacob and, eventually, for the entire Israelite nation. Jacob's statement, "I saw God face to face, and yet my life was spared" (verse 30), indicates he expected that, after seeing the face of God, he would indeed die. But could it be that, rather than dying physically, Jacob "died to self"?

Did he finally learn that he and his offspring would flourish not by means of his own self-sufficiency, schemes, and skill, but by depending upon God and God alone?

Sometimes, to get our attention, God reaches down into time as we know it and interjects his infinite presence into our finite world. In this story God directly intervened with his creature Jacob by calling him to intimate interaction and deep change. When Jacob finally did follow his family across the river, it was a significantly different man who waded through the water!

MAKING IT REAL

8. For years God allowed Jacob to believe that his own schemes and abilities were the reasons for his success. Until this night. It's as though God finally said, "Enough!" firmly showing Jacob that "I am in control." In what situations have you mistakenly believed that you were in control of your life? How has God shown you otherwise? What did he do to get your attention? Do you need to recognize and admit his sovereignty right now?

⟋ 9. Describe a specific time from your past when you discovered how useless it is to struggle with God. What caused you to give up your struggle? What did you learn from that experience?

10. Earlier we suggested that Jacob "must have been aware that he was completely at this Being's mercy and could offer him nothing." Describe specific ways in which you find yourself in this same position. Does accepting that you are at God's mercy give you peace or lead you to panic? Explain. (Try to be completely honest in your response.)

FOUR

"WHAT IS THAT IN YOUR HAND?"

EXODUS 3:1–4:17

*Moses answered, "What if they do not believe me or listen to me
and say, 'The LORD did not appear to you'?"*
Then the LORD said to him, "What is that in your hand?"
"A staff," he replied.

—EXODUS 4:1-2

DRIFTING BABY IN BASKET RESCUED FROM NILE RIVER!
HEBREW WAIF ADOPTED AS EGYPTIAN ROYALTY
PHARAOH'S SON SLAYS EGYPTIAN! MURDERER STILL AT LARGE

Were we to describe Moses' early years in a newspaper, these headlines
would all be accurate. All this, and he was still only about forty years old!
Even before God met him in the desert, Moses had lived anything but an
ordinary life.

As a baby Moses was put in a basket and then tenderly placed in the
Nile River; in this way, his mother hoped to save him from the Egyptian
pharaoh's edict that all Hebrew baby boys should be put to death. Then,
while watching over him as he floated among the reeds, Moses' sister saw

Pharaoh's daughter find him. Pharaoh's daughter immediately recognized Moses as a Hebrew, and yet she still chose to adopt him as her very own. As if that weren't enough of a miracle, at the suggestion of Moses' sister, Pharaoh's daughter agreed to allow the baby to be nursed by a Hebrew woman—none other than Moses' own mother! God's hand was obviously upon Moses from the moment of his birth.

Wouldn't you assume that, with such a background, Moses would have become a courageous and natural leader, full of confidence in his abilities and eager to use those gifts? You might. But that was not an accurate picture of Moses—at least not yet! When God appeared to him as a burning bush and announced that he was sending Moses to lead the Israelites out of bondage in Egypt, Moses pretty much cowered. Came up with excuses. And finally begged God to simply send someone else.

Maybe you've heard the familiar "bookend" stories of Moses. First is the tender account of the baby in a basket. Then much later is the adventure-filled rendition of the ten plagues and the miraculous parting of the Red Sea in which the Israelites crossed over on dry land; they were led by a courageous Moses who raised his shepherd's staff above the water, faithfully believing that God would indeed save them in their time of need. But in between those stories is the critical but somewhat lesser known tale: the interaction between an insecure Moses and his mighty God. What occurred in this exchange? How could Moses evolve from a man of excuses into a man of such incredible faith and courage?

Deep change often comes after a simple yet profound interaction with God, and the growth that took place in Moses' life was no exception.

BREAKING GROUND

Think of a time when someone asked you to do something that made you hesitate out of lack of confidence or fear. What was asked of you? Did you eventually attempt that task? Would you respond differently to that request now? If so, how?

Think back to your elementary, high-school, or college years. Can you recall a time when you didn't want to do something that was required of you, so you made up an excuse to escape facing the truth? For example, did you ever claim to be sick to avoid going to school to give an oral presentation, take a test, or turn in an assignment you hadn't completed? As you think back on that time now, were you attempting to cover up feelings of insecurity about your abilities? Explain.

Read Exodus 3:1–4:17.

THE FLAMING BUSH THAT DIDN'T BURN

Since out-of-the-ordinary events seemed to follow Moses everywhere, he probably should have quickly recognized that he was not destined to live a tranquil life! After fleeing Egypt because he had committed a crime (albeit a courageous one), Moses and his new wife, Zipporah, settled into a relatively calm and quiet life. But that was not to last long. At the start of Exodus 3, Moses was minding his own business, tending the sheep of his father-in-law, Jethro, when God once again directly intervened in the affairs of men—and in Moses' affairs in particular.

Seeing a bush that was on fire but miraculously not consumed, Moses was curious and drew closer for a better look. God called to him from the bush, and Moses quickly responded, "Here I am" (3:4). After telling Moses to remove his sandals since he was standing on "holy ground" (3:5), the Lord began to explain his plan and Moses' part in it: Because of the oppression of his people, God was "sending [Moses] to Pharaoh to bring my people the Israelites out of Egypt" (3:10). But God had only just concluded his instructions when Moses interjected with a question. And the first of many excuses.

Read aloud the litany of Moses' complaints from chapters 3 and 4, and you'll probably note a crescendo of whining as you work through the list!

- "Who am I, that I should go to Pharaoh?" (3:11)
- "Suppose I go to the Israelites and say to them, 'The God of your fathers has sent me to you,' and they ask me, 'What is his name?' Then what shall I tell them?" (3:13)
- "What if they do not believe me or listen to me and say, 'The LORD did not appear to you'?" (4:1)
- "O Lord, I have never been eloquent, neither in the past nor since you have spoken to your servant. I am slow of speech and tongue" (4:10).
- "O Lord, please send someone else to do it" (4:13).

With each question or excuse, God responded to Moses with graciousness and loving assurance, showing serious consideration for Moses' concerns by offering thorough and patient answers. But when Moses asked,

"What if they do not believe me?" (4:1)—implying that the Israelites would never trust him because of his background—God finally answered with a question.

"What is that in your hand?" (4:2) he asked. Direct and simple. Or maybe not so simple? Still, God had promised he would help Moses convince the Israelites that he was indeed God's emissary. Promising even more than his presence (although that should have sufficed), God now showed Moses that by throwing his staff on the ground, it would miraculously become a writhing snake. And how did Moses respond? He ran! When God then told him to grab the snake by the tail—an act that would take courage on Moses' part because of his obvious fears—the snake became a staff once again (4:4).

Finally, God showed Moses other supernatural ways to demonstrate his authority to the Israelites: Moses watched as his own hand become leprous and then healed when he simply slipped it in and out of his cloak (4:6-7). God also instructed Moses to pour water from the Nile River onto dry ground. "The water...will become blood," he promised (4:9).

You would think that these signs, combined with the miracles Moses could perform with the staff, would fully convince him that he was up to the task. He certainly had all he needed to lead the people, including this all-important provision: God's very real presence to guide and direct him. But Moses still wasn't convinced. Are you getting the impression that Moses wasn't the superhuman, Hollywood type of hero? Evidently that's not the only kind of person God can use!

First Looks

1. God's compassion for Israel was apparent when he first explained why he had "come down" to earth—or once again directly interjected his supernatural presence into our finite

world. What phrases in 3:7-10 point to God's empathy for his people? How do they show him to be a personal and loving God?

2. Consider Moses' background: his birth, the circumstances surrounding his adoption, his education and associations with the Egyptians. What advantages might those circumstances have given him? What gifts and abilities might he have developed because of his remarkable upbringing?

3. In 3:18-22, God made one promise concerning the elders of Israel and four promises concerning the Egyptians. What were these promises? What proof do we find in chapter 4 that Moses doubted at least one promise?

Read Exodus 4:1-17 again.

When God Says, "Enough!"

In Exodus 3:18, God succinctly stated, "The elders of Israel will listen to you." But only a few verses later, Moses asked, "What if they don't believe me or listen to me?" (4:1). Looking at those phrases without any intervening text starkly illustrates God's great patience with Moses. But after God demonstrated his power by means of the staff, the leprous hand, and the promise that the water of the Nile would turn to blood, his forbearance appeared to have reached its limit.

Moses then subtly switched his tactics to his personal shortcomings: He decided to get more specific, complaining that his speaking ability was not adequate for this calling. God's reply was quite clear. He quickly set limits for the excuses he would tolerate from Moses and strongly implied (through rhetorical questions) that, as Creator, he is the giver of every human ability. We can hear a touch of anger (or impatience?) as God asserted that *he alone* gives the ability to speak. The ability to hear. The ability to see. And then with the promise of his help—"I will help you speak and will teach you what to say" (4:12)—God sent Moses on his way to do what he had commanded.

At that point, the interaction appeared to be over. Moses had worked through his concerns, worries, and inadequacies. God had answered each with a patience and thoroughness that clearly demonstrated his love for this timid patriarch. You would think Moses would have taken the hint to get a grip, move on, and begin the task God called him to do! Yet Moses refused to give up and, pushing God beyond tolerable limits, he made one final plea: "O Lord, please send someone else to do it" (4:13).

When you were a child and had pushed your parents beyond their endurance, did your mom or dad sometimes announce with great frustration, "That's *enough!*" That appears to have been pretty much God's response to Moses. We read that "the LORD's anger burned against Moses" (4:14). We can only wonder—did the tenor and tone of God's voice change to reflect that anger? In response, did Moses cower in fear? Did he realize that he had finally gone just a bit too far? We can only speculate, but one thing is apparent: That was Moses' last comment!

TAKING IT IN

4. In response to Moses' first two questions (3:11,13), God answered in an unusual way: He described himself. What did he say about his character? How did those answers speak to the heart of Moses' concerns?

5. Describe as best you can the meaning of God's name for himself: "I AM WHO I AM" (3:14). Why does the shortened version—"I AM"—also encompass all that God is?

6. You've probably seen Egyptian hieroglyphics that picture one of the most venomous of snakes, the cobra. Because this snake symbolized life and power to the Egyptians, it is significant that God used it as a miraculous sign. What would Moses' actions

(changing the staff into a snake and then back again) have communicated about God to the Egyptians?

Read Exodus 4:1-5,14-17 again.

ONE ORDINARY SHEPHERD'S STAFF

Apparently, God takes great delight in this simple plan: He chooses an ordinary person, asks him or her to do an extraordinary task, gifts this person with the necessary abilities, and then sends the adventurer on his or her way. And he includes an invaluable bonus: He promises never to leave the one he sends. Care to guess who's included in that simple yet amazing design? *You!*

Consider Moses' staff. An unadorned stick with a hook on one end. Probably carved by the shepherd himself. Rough. Simple. Practical. Handy to lean upon. Useful for guiding the sheep or chasing away an impending threat. Now picture that staff gripped firmly in Moses' hand as he approached the burning bush. At that point the shepherd's staff wasn't anything exceptional. You wouldn't have thought it extraordinary in any way—until God asked the question, "What is that in your hand?"

Suddenly, the ordinary became extraordinary as God used that basic tool in the scope of his great plan. Using one man's faith and courage—and the one simple possession that Moses brought with him to the bush—God would lead the nation of Israel into the Promised Land and would eventually bring forth the Messiah from her line! No matter how small…no matter how simple…no matter how ordinary, unimportant, or deficient you perceive the gifts you bring to God, rest in this truth: They are *enough*.

God called Moses to accomplish an incredible task. And he still calls each of us to assume a role—and to accomplish tasks—in his kingdom today. The question, "What is that in your hand?" forces us to evaluate our lives and ask ourselves, Is God asking me to do something right now that I'm finding excuses not to do? What gifts has he given me to accomplish my tasks for his kingdom? Am I being a good steward of the gifts he has given me for a specific reason? As you reflect on these questions, remember that God is never wasteful. He doesn't give gifts that are inadequate, deficient, or unusable. And he certainly doesn't intend for those gifts to lie dormant.

God asked, "What is that in your hand?"

"A staff" was the succinct reply.

One ordinary staff. One big God. And one timid follower willing to accomplish the task set before him. So take heart and be courageous! Step forward to the bush. God has a question for you.

MAKING IT REAL

7. Why do you think God asked the question, "What is that in your hand?" Why didn't he state, "You have a staff. I will use it to help the Israelites believe that I have sent you." What benefit is there—for Moses and for us—in being asked a question rather than merely hearing a statement?

8. Imagine that God has just asked you the same question: "What is that in your hand?" What is your calling to contribute to his kingdom? What gifts and abilities do you bring to him to accomplish those tasks? Does your gift involve using a pen or the mouse connected to your computer? the ability to give financially? Or is it a beautiful voice? showing hospitality in your home? using skills from your workplace? What do you have that he can use to work his will?

9. While growing up in Pharaoh's household, Moses gained an education, knowledge of Egyptian history, and an understanding of both Egyptian and Israelite cultures. All of that was preparing Moses to be used by God in a unique way. In what ways is this same process evident in your own life? Describe a time in your life when God used one of your "ordinary" gifts or abilities in an extraordinary way.

10. What task do you believe God is currently asking you to do? If you're not presently using your gifts to serve God in that way, what's stopping you? How does God's promise to "never leave you" (Deuteronomy 31:6) give you the courage to step out of your comfort zone and allow him to use you?

11. Consider prayerfully how God's love is evident in his gifts to you. Moses and the Israelites needed to learn that God is a personal and loving God rather than One to be feared. How can the truth of God's love directly affect your ability to move beyond your insecurities and fears and trust him more fully?

FIVE

"WHY HAVE YOU BEATEN YOUR DONKEY?"

NUMBERS 22:20-41

Then the LORD opened Balaam's eyes, and he saw the angel of the LORD standing in the road with his sword drawn. So he bowed low and fell facedown.

The angel of the LORD asked him, "Why have you beaten your donkey these three times? I have come here to oppose you because your path is a reckless one before me."

—NUMBERS 22:31-32

Do you ever talk to your pet? Our guess is that most people do. As dog owners we certainly repeat phrases like "Sit up!" or "Play dead!" or even "Fetch the paper!" (That last command is handy only if the paper makes it to you in one piece.) So talking to an animal is not at all unusual. But have you ever heard an animal *answer* you? Now that's an entirely different scenario!

In this study, however, we'll read about a two-sided conversation between a man and an animal—and like many two-sided conversations, it gets a little confused. As we know, miscommunication in conversation often happens when the receiver doesn't hear the message correctly, when the sender's words are garbled, when nonverbal messages are misunderstood, or when the sender and receiver simply have no chance to understand each other because of a language difference or cultural gap. If you've ever tried to communicate with someone who spoke another language, you quickly learned that pantomiming leaves much to be desired!

Now think back to your teen years. How often did you and your parents experience bungled communication? Fairly regularly? Think especially of those times when your parents' rules and messages seemed unfair. Instead of truly understanding the motivations behind their decrees, you misconstrued their intentions and reacted with anger. Essentially, you weren't able to see the motivating love behind their messages, and you probably resisted by talking back, arguing, or even rebelling. But now—in hindsight—you understand that those rules and decrees were designed to protect or teach you.

The story we're about to read contains all those elements: miscommunication, disobedience, hidden motivations—and even a talking animal.

BREAKING GROUND

Describe a time when your motivations to help or protect someone were misconstrued and misjudged. Did it involve your spouse? a friend? someone in your workplace? or maybe your children? How did it feel to be misunderstood?

Were you eventually able to show the other person that your motives were in his or her best interest? How did that person then respond?

Read Numbers 22:20-41.

What a Prince Requested

When the Israelites were in obedience to their God as they marched through the yet-to-be-conquered Promised Land, they were an imposing force. Whenever the Lord said, "I have handed them over to you" (concerning a tribe that occupied the land), victory was assured, decisive, and swift. So it's no surprise that the reputation of the Israelites and their God preceded them when they traveled to the plains of Moab. They were about to cause a stir again!

Balak, the son of Zippor, who was king of Moab, didn't realize that Israel had no intention of attacking his people. Instead, the Israelites were focused on another prize: Canaan. But when Balak glimpsed the army camped along the Jordan River, he reacted to the Israelites' presence with near panic. Quickly realizing that his tribe (the Moabites) had no chance of defeating this fearsome enemy in battle, he sought alternative means to save his people: He called upon Balaam, a pagan diviner (or sorcerer) who had an international reputation for success. In the past—or so Balak believed—anyone Balaam cursed was doomed. So Balak sent his messengers to bring back this famous man. Balaam was to put a curse on the Israelites, assuring the Moabites of victory.

Surprisingly, Balaam responded to the messengers by telling them that they must spend the night while he sought the Lord's will in the matter. Balaam was evidently quite agreeable to cursing the Israelites, but when he brought the matter to God, God's answer was quick and definitive: He informed Balaam that he was not to go with the Moabites—"You must not put a curse on those people [the Israelites], because they are blessed" (Numbers 22:12). So the messengers returned to Balak empty-handed.

Later, when Balak once again attempted to persuade Balaam to change his mind—sending "princes, more numerous and more distinguished than the first" (22:15)—God spoke to Balaam a second time. With one major directive—"Do only what I tell you" (22:20)—he allowed Balaam to go. What might have been Balaam's intention as he set off on this journey? Did he plan to do what God said? Or was he determined to fulfill Balak's request?

God was about to intervene in the affairs of humanity yet again, and in an imaginative way! For no matter what others may have had in mind, God was intent upon working his ultimate will as he directed both the Israelites and the pagan peoples with whom they came into contact. No mere diviner or curse could ever prevent God from molding a nation from which would come the One with the power to abolish sin's curse forever: Jesus the Messiah!

FIRST LOOKS

1. In response to the messengers' request, the diviner Balaam responded, "I will bring you back the answer the LORD gives me" (22:8). A diviner seeking the Lord's will? What other antithetical statements did Balaam make in the first twenty verses of

chapter 22? What do you think accounts for the contradiction between this man's beliefs and his actions?

2. God's directive to Balaam in verse 20 was crystal clear: "Go with them, but do only what I tell you." And yet God's initial reaction to Balaam's departure with the princes was intense anger (verse 22). What does this suggest about Balaam's intentions?

3. The dumb beast, a donkey, saw the Angel of the Lord in the road. The diviner, supposedly a deeply spiritual man, was completely blind to the angel's presence! How many more times did this scenario happen before God "opened Balaam's eyes" (verse 31)? What actually happened to Balaam when his eyes were "opened"?

Read Numbers 22:21-31 again.

WHAT A DONKEY SAW

The journey had begun. Balaam and the princes had saddled up and were on their way, with God's blessing. But it wasn't long before the Lord manifested his absolute opposition to this quest, for Christ himself in preincarnate form blocked their way, a drawn sword in his hand.[3] We're told emphatically that the Angel of the Lord "stood in the road to oppose him" (verse 22). So who was it that saw and then immediately reacted to this manifestation? Not Balaam. It was the donkey who stopped—and then promptly received a beating for protecting Balaam!

As Balaam attempted to continue on his journey, two more times the donkey backed away from Christ in this threatening form. The third and final time, she went so far as to lie down. The poor beast had nowhere to turn; she was caught between an angry man and an even angrier God! At this point in the story, God miraculously gifted the donkey with a way to vent her frustration. We're told that "the LORD opened the donkey's mouth, and she said to Balaam, 'What have I done to you to make you beat me these three times?'" (verse 28).

Balaam's response was amazing. Amazing not just because he was embarrassed and angry enough to wish right then for a sword to kill his donkey, but because he didn't seem surprised that his donkey actually talked to him! Was Balaam so angry and focused on himself that he disregarded the miraculous? Or was this a common occurrence for a man who practiced sorcery? Whatever the reason, God once again displayed an appreciation for irony in Balaam's desire for a sword. There was indeed a sword nearby, but it was being wielded by an angry God—and it was directed toward Balaam himself!

---

3. See note on page 20 for information regarding the preincarnate Christ.

Next, the donkey tried to reason with Balaam, pointing out that she was "your own donkey, which you have always ridden" and asking, "Have I been in the habit of doing this to you?" (verse 30). When Balaam reluctantly confessed "no," we're told that "the LORD opened Balaam's eyes" (verse 31). Whenever we find parallel structures in Scripture, we need to take special note of them. When we compare the phrase "the LORD opened the donkey's mouth" (verse 28) with the phrase "the LORD opened Balaam's eyes" (verse 31), it seems clear that God was always in control, no matter what Balaam might have assumed.

But *finally* Balaam reacted in a way that was expected; he "bowed low and fell facedown" (verse 31). (This is somehow satisfying to those of us who appreciate fairness and justice in this world!) Could it be that Balaam was ready to listen? to truly *see* for the first time?

Taking It In

4. In the Old Testament, the Angel of the Lord was always a human manifestation of God—or Christ—in preincarnate form (see note on page 20). Why do you think God himself met Balaam here rather than sending an angel?

5. It appears that God contradicted himself—or, at the very least, changed his mind—when he gave Balaam permission to go to Balak and then stopped him. If we focus on God's one directive to Balaam when he told him to go—"do only what I tell you,"

(verse 20)—what does this suggest about his anger at Balaam in verse 22? What "hidden" motivations and purposes might Balaam have had that were obvious to God?

⚔ 6. What conclusions can we draw from the fact that the Angel of the Lord was *visible* to the dumb beast but *invisible* to Balaam the diviner? What implications might that have for us as we seek God's will?

7. What significance do you see in the Holy Spirit's parallel use of "the LORD opened the donkey's mouth" (verse 28) and "the LORD opened Balaam's eyes" (verse 31)? Do you think one of the miracles was greater? If so, which one? Why?

Read Numbers 22:32-41 again.

What a Sorcerer Discovered

God asked Balaam yet another penetrating query that remains timeless in its scope and deeper meaning: "Why have you beaten your donkey?" (verse 32). When Balaam was asked that question, he was forced to look at many issues in his life: his hidden motives; his anger, which was released on an innocent animal; and his disregard for God's ability to fulfill his ultimate plan for his own people, Israel. As we read God's question today, we're called to address some of the same issues.

When Balaam's eyes were finally opened, he saw Christ, sword in hand. But after the Lord's probing question and insightful observations, Balaam was forced to "see" much more. He recognized and acknowledged his sin. He confessed his ignorance. He was willing to turn around, reverse his course of action, and immediately head home. But our forgiving God was willing to give Balaam another chance and, once again, sent him on his way with the instruction, "Go with the men, but speak only what I tell you" (verse 35).

Just where are you on your journey? Is it time to ask the Lord to open your eyes so you can truly see?

Making It Real

8. Our deepest motivations are often hidden, difficult to uncover, and slippery because they act like chameleons, changing to fit the situation. But even though our motivations may be buried deep within our hearts, they are not concealed from God. What wrong motivations do you need to admit to yourself? to God?

9. The Angel of the Lord blocked Balaam's path, telling him to stop his "reckless" actions (verse 32). Has God been telling you to stop an action, change an attitude, or reconsider a decision, but you've been refusing to "see"? What do you need to do to change this situation? Do you need to go in a totally different direction? Or has God told you to follow him in a specific way? Are you following?

10. Sometimes we are blind to God's unseen hand of protection on our lives, such as when a trip is suddenly cancelled or an unhealthy relationship ends. Have you ever had such an experience but didn't realize it until afterward? How did you initially respond to God's protection? Do you think you might respond differently in the future?

11. Even though you desire to obey God, do you find it difficult to obey when it is emotionally costly? In what ways, if any, have you knowingly fought against God's will? Have you ever fought

against God's will subconsciously and then become aware of what you were doing? Explain.

12. This story about Balak and Balaam demonstrates that God sometimes does the unexpected. Has God ever done something unexpected in your life—good or bad—that he used to help you grow in your relationship with him? Explain.

13. Since Christ's death and resurrection, we've moved from living under the bondage of the law to experiencing freedom in his grace. Yet the New Testament is filled with commands against sin that are intended to protect us: We shouldn't cling to our anger rather than forgive; we shouldn't have sex outside of marriage; we shouldn't love money. Can you think of some other commands that are also for our protection? What effect has this kind of protection had on you personally?

14. In 2 Peter 2:15-16, Peter referred to Balaam when he warned against false teachers who had infiltrated the church. Listing their sinful actions with great passion, Peter cited Balaam as an example of one who "loved the wages of wickedness" (verse 15). If you can, give some present-day examples of unscrupulous men or women who exploit the church, taking Christians' money for sinful reasons. What does Peter's message say to us about how we should handle offerings given to our churches?

"WHAT ARE YOU DOING DOWN ON YOUR FACE?"

JOSHUA 7:1-26

"O Lord, what can I say, now that Israel has been routed by its ene-mies? The Canaanites and the other people of the country will hear about this and they will surround us and wipe out our name from the earth. What then will you do for your own great name?"

The LORD said to Joshua, "Stand up! What are you doing down on your face?"

—JOSHUA 7:8-10

Accepting blame is tough to do. Like children caught cheating in a game, we are often eager to point fingers elsewhere rather than admit our own culpability. I (Carolyn) can recall a time my classmates and I were told to play 7-Up while our teacher made a quick trip to the office. When she returned to discover the class in total chaos, no one had the courage to admit that he or she had created the discord. Many of us had cheated, peeking to see who was "it"—and that definitely included me!

Though the "games" become more complex as we grow older, each passing decade shows that we are still reluctant to admit our guilt. As teens, how many of us used the excuse, "But all my friends did it"? That blanket it's-therefore-really-not-my-fault rationale may have covered anything from slipping under a roped area to see a movie for free to copying a friend's homework. Or it might have been used to justify more serious actions such as shoplifting or experimenting with drugs. By the time we reach our adult years, we're still childishly pointing fingers elsewhere: at work ("My assistant didn't get the work sheet to me on time, so it's *her* fault I was late"), in the community ("The voting lines were too long! If those people at the polls had been more organized, I would have voted."), in our relationships ("You were inconsiderate, so it's *your* fault that I got angry and lost my temper!"), and even in the church ("That pastor's not a very good teacher, so it's *his* fault I'm not growing spiritually.").

Unfortunately, biblical patriarchs weren't immune to this tendency either. As faithful as Joshua was—trusting his God to lead the Israelites into mighty battles to possess the Promised Land—he was also quick to deflect blame when an invasion failed. At one point Joshua cried out, "Ah, Sovereign LORD, why did *you* ever bring this people across the Jordan to deliver us into the hands of the Amorites to destroy us?" (verse 7, emphasis added). Translation: "If you hadn't brought us here, God, we wouldn't have this problem." No wonder the Lord answered him with a direct, concise command!

BREAKING GROUND

Describe a time when, as a child or a teenager, you were guilty of some sort of offense but blamed another person for it.

Why were you afraid to accept responsibility? If possible, describe what you felt at the time.

Read Joshua 7:1-26.

No Thrill of Victory

Fresh from their tremendous victory at Jericho, the people of Israel turned their attention toward the next town to be conquered: Ai. Just as he had done years before, Joshua sent out scouts to "spy out the region" (verse 2). When the scouts returned, their confidence in God and his ability to give them another victory was evident. They boastfully told Joshua, "Not all the people will have to go up against Ai. Send [only] two or three thousand men to take it" (verse 3).

But Joshua and the Israelites were about to receive a shock. Instead of the flush of victory they had expected, they experienced defeat: "They were routed by the men of Ai, who killed about thirty-six of them" (verses 4-5). We can sense their discouragement when we read that "the hearts of the people melted and became like water" (verse 5). In the past these words had been used to describe the pagan Canaanites. But now they described the defeated, dejected, and weary nation of Israel and its courageous leader, Joshua.

At this point we need to backtrack a bit to discover the cause of this devastating defeat. Verse 1 informs us that there was willful sin among the Israelites; Achan had violated God's firm command that no booty was ever to be taken from conquered peoples for personal gain (see Joshua 6:18).

Because Achan had taken things for himself, God's "anger burned against Israel" (verse 1). Israel's fortunes took a tremendous blow between the last verse of chapter 6 that tells us "the LORD was with Joshua, and his fame spread throughout the land" and the beginning of chapter 7, which opens with the ominous word *but*. The consequences of sin came swiftly.

Though only one man had sinned, it's apparent that God considered the entire nation guilty—apparently, members of Achan's family were also aware of the stolen goods and knew where they were hidden inside his tent. Since goods claimed from a victory were to go into the Lord's treasury, Achan had essentially stolen *from God*. The magnitude of the consequences Israel experienced because of this sin show that God viewed his covenant people in a corporate sense. He would not tolerate this sin of stealing devoted things. Not by many. Not by a few. And not even by one. Either the nation of Israel obeyed...or they suffered defeat.

FIRST LOOKS

1. What evidence, if any, can you find that Joshua or the spies sought God's direction before they went to spy out Ai? before they went into battle? In the previous chapter the nation of Israel had easily won the battle of Jericho. How might that victory have affected how they approached the battle with Ai?

2. What words or phrases spoken by the Israelites might indicate a presumptuous attitude toward a guaranteed victory over Ai? What evidence suggests that the spies were overly confident? How did they underrate Ai's abilities?

3. How did the Israelites respond physically when they were defeated? How did they respond emotionally?

Read Joshua 7:6-15 again.

No Defense for the Guilty

After Israel's defeat, Joshua and the elders immediately began to display all the formal signs of mourning: They fell on their faces before the ark of the Lord, tore their clothes, and sprinkled dust on their heads. Although this was the expected ritual for mourning the loss of life—they had lost thirty-six men—their motivations for the ritual appear to have gone much deeper. Joshua expressed the feelings of the entire nation when he woefully cried out, "Ah, Sovereign LORD, why did you ever bring this people across the Jordan to deliver us into the hands of the Amorites to destroy us?"

(verse 7). He appeared to be stunned, shocked, crushed by the defeat, for he wondered at God's apparent abandonment.

Joshua went on to ask God two more questions: "O Lord, what can I say, now that Israel has been routed by its enemies?" (verse 8) and "What then will you do for your own great name?" (verse 9). Ironically, even though Joshua made an outward show of seeking God through mourning and repentance, all three of his questions implied that the Lord (and the Lord alone) was responsible for the Israelites' defeat:

Why did *you* lead us across the Jordan River?

Why did *you* allow us to be routed by our enemies?

Why did *you* permit your reputation ("your own great name") to be damaged?

In each case, Joshua assumed no responsibility for their loss, which he referred to as a rout (verse 8). Even though he had stretched out in a prostrate position of humility and submission before the Lord—remember that he was facedown on the ground—his spirit and attitude appeared to be anything but humble! Or had Joshua deluded himself into believing that God would offer only sympathy and not punishment?

Whatever Joshua was feeling at that time, God's response to him and all the elders was succinct and direct: "Stand up! What are you doing down on your face?" (verse 10). If Joshua and the nation of Israel were expecting God to bless and reward them for their "humble" response, they were certainly taken by surprise once again. For God appeared to be saying to them, "If you're really contrite, do something about the sin that caused this failure!" God proceeded to count off Israel's sins: "They have violated my covenant...taken some of the devoted things...stolen...lied" and "put them with their own possessions" (verse 11).

The Lord didn't waste time in moving to the remedy either. After instructing the Israelites to "destroy whatever among you is devoted to destruction" (verse 12), he called on them to consecrate themselves and then prepare to present themselves to him tribe by tribe. In this way, most likely by drawing lots, the family "that the LORD takes shall come forward man by man. He who is caught with the devoted things shall be destroyed by fire, along with all that belongs to him" (verses 14-15). The Judge of the Earth had pronounced the laws broken, presented the evidence, and announced the verdict. Sentencing of the guilty party would soon begin.

TAKING IT IN

4. Why do you think Joshua and the elders would consider a loss of thirty-six men a rout? What implications had they drawn from the loss? What judgments was the nation of Israel making about God that were not true? What judgments were true?

5. Joshua was greatly concerned about the Lord's—and the Israelites'—reputation and honor. What did he seem to be inferring when he said, "The Canaanites and the other people of the country...will wipe out our name from the earth. What then will you do for your own great name?" (verse 9). What was Joshua concerned about regarding "our name" and the Lord's "great name"?

6. The word *stand* is repeated three times in verses 10-13 (emphasis added).

   Stand up! (verse 10)

   That is why the Israelites cannot *stand* against their enemies. (verse 12)

   You cannot *stand* against your enemies until you remove [the devoted things]. (verse 13)

   What meaning can we draw from the repetition of this word? Why do you think God told the Israelites to stand and then informed them why they could not stand?

7. Obviously, God knew all along that Achan was the guilty party. Why then do you think that God asked Joshua and the people to go through the long process of identifying the sinner? What was gained by having each family step forward?

Read Joshua 7:16-26 again.

NO PLEA TO BE BARGAINED

Early the next morning Joshua began the process that God had established to reveal the guilty party. Though it appeared to be a random selection process, it definitely was not: God directly controlled the system. When Achan was picked, Joshua confronted him with a parental "My son, give glory to the LORD... Tell me what you have done; do not hide it from me" (verse 19). Achan's response—finally someone admitted responsibility!—was to acknowledge, "It is true! I have sinned against the LORD, the God of Israel" (verse 20).

But was Achan's admission too little, too late? Evidently. For once the stolen booty was found in Achan's tent, Joshua and all of Israel stoned Achan and the other members of his family—and later burned their bodies. If we think that response was too harsh and without mercy, then we need to read again God's decree in verse 15: "He who is caught with the devoted things shall be destroyed by fire.... He has violated the covenant of the LORD and has done a disgraceful thing in Israel!" God's holiness, justice, and law were being demonstrated and taught through this interaction with his people, and the Lord apparently saw the need to state unequivocally and deliberately: "You must obey me completely, for I will *not* be taken lightly."

What if Achan had stepped forward the previous night and admitted his guilt? Would God have forgiven him? That calls for mere speculation, and the truth is, we'll never know. But at the same time, we can list other Old Testament people who needed God's mercy and forgiveness and received them in abundance: Abraham, Sarah, Jacob, Rahab, and Moses. We dare not point a finger at God for not being merciful, when we're the ones who need to take responsibility for our sins and acknowledge our guilt.

MAKING IT REAL

8. How have you treated lightly what God considers most serious? What were the results?

9. When God asked Joshua, "What are you doing down on your face?" he seemed to be saying that repentance involves much more than mere words and misplaced emotions. He appeared to be calling Joshua to action ("Stand up!") and a drastic change in behavior. But sometimes we are paralyzed by sin in our lives. If the idea of drastic change feels overwhelming, we might be tempted to stay "on our faces." In what ways have you been paralyzed? In which areas of your life do you need to "stand up"?

10. When, if ever, have you been guilty of acting repentant and humble before God when in reality you continued to hide a rebellious and stubborn spirit? What can you do to seek God's will—rather than your own—as you repent of your sin? If you

have merely verbalized your need to change at this point, what can you do to turn those words into action?

11. True repentance involves specific steps. For example, if we have lied, we need to stop lying, admit that we have lied, ask forgiveness for lying, and then begin telling the truth. What steps do you need to take toward repentance?

12. Think of a time when, as an adult, you needed to accept responsibility for wrongdoing but instead blamed another person. Do you need to apologize to someone? What do you need to do to make things right?

SEVEN

"AM I NOT SENDING YOU?"

JUDGES 6:1-29

The LORD turned to him and said, "Go in the strength you have and save Israel out of Midian's hand. Am I not sending you?"

—JUDGES 6:14

Did you have a nickname when you were growing up? Whether or not you care to acknowledge it might depend on whether you had a nice nickname or a derogatory one. Children can be brutal when it comes to labeling their peers. Names that lend themselves to rhyming are quickly targeted (Lyin' Ryan, for example). People who have, shall we say, "noticeable features" are saddled with constant painful reminders (like Bigfoot Becky). And those with names that have an unfortunate connection to other objects usually don't appreciate their peers' creativity. (Guys named John, for example, don't stand a chance!)

Hopefully, your parents counterbalanced any unpleasant nicknames your peers gave you by using positive labels in your home, ones that affirmed your gifts and encouraged you to develop those abilities for God as you grew older. One of our sons, for example, has always been incredibly service-oriented and loves to help others; we repeatedly praised him for that and emphasized how God would use that quality when he became an adult. Now he's using that desire to help in numerous ways in his church and community. Our other son demonstrated empathetic sensitivity to the plight of others even as a small child. Today he plans to use that gift as he prepares to practice law in a courtroom, viewing his work with clients as a ministry in which he helps hurting people change their lives.

If for some reason you didn't grow up in a home where you received encouraging and positive labels from your parents, take heart! *God the Father—Abba, Father!—views you as his very own child,* and his nicknames for you are exclusively labels of love. If you've accepted Christ as your Savior, God considers you his fully adopted son or daughter, with all the benefits and privileges of being his child. And because of what Jesus Christ did in your stead, God's labels for you now include *holy, washed, righteous,* and *gifted,* which means he's given you abilities to complete the tasks he has called you to do.

Evidently, Gideon needed a boost from God too, an encouraging word to begin the awesome task that God had called him to. Though Gideon was not initially known for his bravery, courage, inspired incentive, or fighting skills, the Angel of the Lord (Christ in preincarnate form) called him a "mighty warrior." As a matter of fact, the very first words Christ uttered to Gideon were full of support, encouragement, and love, for he greeted him with "The LORD is with you, mighty warrior!" (verse 12).

Let's discover how God's question to Gideon asks us to remember who *we* really are.

Breaking Ground

What are some of the nicknames you called your friends in school? Did you have a nickname? Why do you think you called others by their nicknames? How did that make you feel?

Read Judges 6:1-29.

By Way of Introduction

The Israelites constantly repeated this cycle: (1) They turned from God to worship the idols of the pagan people whose land they occupied; (2) God allowed those pagan tribes to make the Israelites' lives miserable; (3) the Israelites cried out to God to save them; (4) they eventually repented and lived under a godly leader for a period of time; only to (5) repeat the cycle again by worshiping idols. No wonder God's anger burned against his chosen people! As we view history from this perspective, it's amazing that, time after time, God graciously rescued and forgave the Israelites.

At the time of this story, the Israelites were on the down side of their recurring pattern: They were worshiping the idols of the Midianites and therefore were under God's judgment. In fact, the text tell us that the "Midianites, Amalekites and other eastern peoples invaded the country...ruined the crops...and did not spare a living thing for Israel, neither sheep nor cattle nor donkeys" (verses 3-4). At this point of desperation, the Israelites "cried out to the LORD for help" (verse 6), but we find no evidence of repentance in their plea. They wanted to be rescued, not judged for their sins.

In response, God first sent a prophet to his wayward people, and this unnamed messenger delivered a statement that was certainly not new to the Israelites: "I am the LORD your God; do not worship the gods of the Amorites, in whose land you live" (verse 10). The prophet finished with this sad summation from God: "But you have not listened to me" (verse 10). What a heartbreaking indictment of any people, let alone God's chosen!

At this point God began actively putting his plan into action. Christ, referred to again as the Angel of the Lord, "came and sat down under the oak...where...Gideon was threshing wheat in a winepress" (verse 11). Gideon's threshing in the winepress might indicate that there was very little wheat to thresh because the Midianites had ravaged the land. And it's clear from the text that he was also concerned that the Midianites might discover what he was doing, so he elected to thresh in a more protected and hidden area.

Can't you just picture the scene? Christ sat under a tree as he leisurely watched Gideon separate the wheat from the chaff. Gideon, intent on finishing the task, probably continued working until the Visitor's startling greeting grabbed his attention. "The LORD is with you, mighty warrior" (verse 12). For such a short salutation, it is packed with meaning! It's important that we take special note of Christ's choice of words here. When he said "with you," he used the singular form of the word *you*, indicating that he was not referring to the entire nation of Israel; instead, he was speaking to Gideon personally.

Though Gideon tried to ignore and parry that explicit reference by asking, "If the LORD is with *us,* why has all this happened to us?" (verse

13, emphasis added), his deflection wasn't about to put off the Lord. God is never distracted or diverted by our attempts to deviate from his will. (Just ask Jonah!)

FIRST LOOKS

1. Through the voice of his prophet, God recounted the many ways he had rescued Israel (verses 7-10). List those examples and then note what the Lord demanded in return. What did he ask of his chosen people above all else?

2. Once again it appears that a sinful people refused to take responsibility for their actions—and clearly brought upon themselves the consequences for those actions. How did Gideon claim not only the Israelites' innocence but also God's culpability for the Midianites' rule over them (verse 13)?

Read Judges 6:14-24 again.

A RELUCTANT HERO

After Gideon finished complaining, the conversation seemed to move to a different level. Either Gideon had continued to work while he listed his grievances in verse 13—which meant that maybe he hadn't yet had eye contact with the Angel of the Lord—or Christ had purposefully moved into Gideon's line of sight to emphasize what he was about to say next. Regardless of what actually occurred, one fact is clear: Christ now acted and spoke with authority. His "Go!" was no suggestion; it was a *command*.

The singular form of the word *you* that was used in verse 12 ("the Lord is with you") was used again in this part of their dialogue. When the Lord told Gideon to "Go in the strength you have" (verse 14), he was referring to his presence in Gideon's life. God was telling Gideon very clearly that he would be strong because God is strong and would be right at his side. Certainly, to be sent on a mission to fight against the Midianite army was one thing; to be sent into battle with Almighty God at one's side was another matter entirely!

We might assume that, when the Lord commissioned Gideon for service, he would have used the imperative again. "Go, for I am sending you!" would have been the most logical charge from God to his servant. That's probably what Gideon expected. Or we might assume that God would have chosen a simple declaration: "I am sending you." But God used this occasion to ask yet another rhetorical question: "Am I not sending you?" (verse 14). This one short query would call Gideon to evaluate where he'd started, where he was going, and with whom.

It's no surprise that this sudden turn of conversation caused Gideon to back-pedal pretty quickly! Whether his response—"My clan is the weakest...and I am the least in my family" (verse 15)—was due to fear, humility, or reality was not important to the Lord. He quickly disregarded that because, as he reminded Gideon yet again, "I will be with you" (verse 16).

Still, Gideon continued his back-pedaling by asking for proof: "If now I have found favor in your eyes, give me a sign that it is really you talking to me" (verse 17). After the Lord reassured Gideon that he would wait for his return, Gideon hurried off to prepare a meal for his guest.

When Gideon returned with food, he probably didn't expect his visitor to touch his staff to the meat and bread so that the food burst into flames. Once the fire had consumed the meal, the Angel of the Lord disappeared. Gideon's tone and response—"Ah, Sovereign LORD! I have seen the angel of the LORD face to face!" (verse 22)—confirmed that he then understood who his visitor had been. He even expected to die because he had seen the Lord face to face.

However, before Gideon could articulate his fears or maybe repeat his list of excuses, the Lord informed him that he would not die. With further reassurances of "Peace! Do not be afraid" (verse 23)—apparently, the Lord spoke to Gideon this time but did not appear to him physically— Gideon built an altar, naming it "The LORD is Peace" (verse 24).

Gideon had been affirmed, called, sent, and provided with proof. Was the reluctant mighty warrior finally prepared to go to battle?

Maybe not.

Taking It In

3. In two direct statements ("The LORD is with you" and "I will be with you") and in two subtle statements ("Go in the strength you have" and "Am I not sending you?"), God reassured Gideon that he would be at his side. In light of this promise, why do you think Gideon still asked for proof?

4. Gideon asked the Lord to stay until he brought him an offering. Why do you think the Lord directed Gideon to put the meat and bread on a rock and pour out the broth?

5. Why do you think Gideon named the location of the altar "The LORD is Peace"? What does this suggest about what Gideon was feeling?

6. God instructed Gideon to use the cut-up Asherah pole as fuel for offering a sacrifice. Also, the sacrificed bull was to come from no other source but the herd of Gideon's father, Joash. What might have been the significance of those two intentional acts for the Israelites? What did this say about God's power?

Read Judges 6:25-29 again.

To Test a Warrior's Courage

The issue at the very heart of Israel's problems was not the Midianites themselves, but the rebellious Israelites' worship of the Midianite gods. So before coming to the rescue of his people once more, God demanded that they destroy the symbol of their sin: the altar to Baal. Ironically, Gideon's own father, Joash, had built this altar. On the night of the Lord's visit to Gideon, God's command to "tear down your father's altar...and cut down the Asherah pole" (verse 25) would obviously present a significant challenge for Gideon.

Yet Gideon did indeed destroy the altar just as God had commanded him. In verse 27 we read that "Gideon took ten of his servants" with him and "did it at night rather than in the daytime" because he was afraid of what his family and the townspeople might do. Before we fault Gideon for acting cowardly, it's important to note: (1) the altar to Baal would have been very large, so having ten servants' help was probably necessary; and (2) if Gideon had attempted this during the day, the people most likely would have stopped him from completing the task. Rather than being a coward who was paralyzed by his fear, Gideon courageously acted in a way that allowed him to do what the Lord asked of him. And remember that this altar belonged to his father. What was an intimidating task in the first place took on even greater significance when that factor was added in!

If you continue reading about Gideon, you'll discover that he did eventually become all that the Lord originally said of him: "The Spirit of the LORD came upon [Gideon]" (verse 34), and he summoned the tribes, eventually leading them to defeat their enemies, the Midianites. Do you suppose the question, "Am I not sending you?" echoed through Gideon's mind as he led the Israelites into battle? Could it be that its deeper meaning encouraged him, giving him the boldness he needed? Would he not have heard in that one simple question the constant reminder from God that affirmed, "*I'm* sending you, *I'm* empowering you, *I'm* right here with you"? Throughout the story of Gideon, we witness God's amazing faithfulness: He kept his promises through his own strength and a human servant.

MAKING IT REAL

7. The Lord verbally reminded Gideon four times that he would be with him. He doesn't often speak with us in that way today, but we do have the Holy Spirit living within us, providing his presence at all times. Describe a time—maybe it was during an unusual or trying situation—when the Holy Spirit assured you of his presence. When, if ever, has God miraculously reminded you of his care, direction, or guidance?

8. Because God views us through the completed work of Jesus Christ on the cross, we stand before him justified. So God saw Gideon's potential as reality when he first greeted him. In other words, God perceived Gideon as a mighty warrior even before

Gideon became one. What potential of yours do you think God might already see as reality?

9. You don't need to lead a nation into battle, travel to another country as a missionary, or practice ministry vocationally to be called by God. Your gifts are evidence of his calling on your life, and you're to use them in your home, church, community, and workplace. In what situations in your life might God ask, "Am I not sending you?" What effect does that rhetorical question have on your view of your gifts and calling?

10. God's question implies, "Since I am sending you, trust in my ability to do what I've called you to do." When God calls you to do something, do you ever find yourself offering excuses about your ability and background, as Gideon did? Explain. What does your response reveal about your view of God?

11. The strength of your calling is based on the fact that *God is the One who authorizes your going.* Others may affirm that calling—family, friends, mentors, churches—but God is the One who sends with authority. How does that knowledge affect your determination to do his will?

EIGHT

"HAVE YOU ANY RIGHT TO BE ANGRY?"

THE BOOK OF JONAH

But Jonah was greatly displeased and became angry. He prayed to the LORD, "O LORD, is this not what I said when I was still at home? That is why I was so quick to flee to Tarshish. I knew that you are a gracious and compassionate God, slow to anger and abounding in love, a God who relents from sending calamity. Now, O LORD, take away my life, for it is better for me to die than to live."
But the LORD replied, "Have you any right to be angry?"
—JONAH 4:1-4

Most of us just want life to be fair. People who are "good" should be rewarded. And those who break the rules should receive judgment and punishment. That's not too much to ask, is it? Apparently so.

Take the guy who illegally passes a long line of cars on the *right* shoulder. The nerve of him! Wouldn't it be wonderful if there were a policeman waiting around the corner to "greet" him? Or how about when a cashier at a discount store—you know the kind: it accommodates two million customers but has only three functioning checkout lanes—opens a new lane. You've been waiting in line for twenty minutes, but someone who has just strolled up to the front of the store makes a mad dash for the newly opened lane, leaving you in the dust. Don't you wish the cashier would let you go first?

Doesn't it drive you crazy when those who do wrong don't "pay" for it? Many of us have known a dishonest businessperson who continues to prosper. Or we've heard about a professional sports figure who breaks the law but hires a high-priced lawyer who gets him off with a small fine. And how about the coworker who flatters her boss with syrupy compliments—and gets the promotion or raise she wants? Where are you when all this is going on? Slaving away at your desk, that's where! How can anyone say that's fair?

Have you noticed, however, that our calls for fair play, justice, and retribution always involve the *other* guy? We want the cheater, the philanderer, the line-cutter, and the guy in the little red sports car who cuts us off to get caught, sentenced, and punished. We aren't calling for judgment on ourselves because *he's* the guilty one and *we're* innocent. Totally. Always. Well, most of the time...

You've heard the expression, "Justice is blind." Maybe it should also be said that justice is "what the other guy deserves." We're quick to point out another person's faults while ignoring our own. We cry out for others to be punished when we're guilty of the same sin, only in a different venue. And our disgust and vehemence at the guilty one's not getting caught is quite self-righteous, especially in light of those times when we do wrong and get away with it. We probably don't put much emotional energy into *those* situations—other than a sigh of relief!

Jonah was no different from us in his desire to see sinners suffer the consequences of their sins. Setting himself up as judge and jury, he condemned the people of the city of Nineveh. In Jonah's opinion, they were guilty as charged and therefore should not be granted mercy. So when God asked his servant to go preach to the people of Nineveh, Jonah's desire for justice, judgment, and retribution was too strong. Afraid that the Ninevites might repent—and knowing that his God was a God of mercy—Jonah skipped town.

He soon learned that hiding from God wasn't quite so simple.

BREAKING GROUND

Describe the last incident you witnessed—possibly in traffic, in a store, or at work—when it seemed to you that a person should have been caught and punished for something, but wasn't. How did that make you feel? If you could have handed down some form of punishment or justice, what would that have looked like, and how do you think you would have felt?

Now think of a time when you got away with an act that was illegal or morally and ethically wrong. Maybe you broke the speed limit, parked in a no-parking zone, or received a lowered price on an article you were purchasing when you knew it wasn't on sale. Were your feelings as intense in this situation as they were in the other situation when the guy didn't get caught? Why do you think your reaction was different (if it was)?

Read the book of Jonah.

A WAYWARD CHILD

When God directly interacted with men or women in the Old Testament, he was attempting to teach them—and us—that he intended to accomplish his plan, no matter what. Whether he used a sorcerer and a talking donkey, a scheming patriarch, or a misguided Hebrew raised by Egyptians, God continually demonstrated his supreme sovereignty, his will, and his determination to bring salvation to all peoples. In the book of Jonah, God once again used a biblical character—and Jonah is a character in every sense of the word!—to do just that.

When we first meet Jonah, God has just given him his marching orders: He was instructed to go to Nineveh and preach to the wicked people there. Jonah's response to that command? He did indeed march, but in the opposite direction! Jonah had already demonstrated that he wasn't about to make anything easy, for we're told that he "ran away from the LORD" (1:3). The fact that Jonah thought he could go someplace where God couldn't find him—and get away with it—tells us a great deal about him.

To be fair to Jonah, we need to take a closer look at the relationship between the nation of Israel and city of Nineveh. God himself mentioned the city's wickedness in Jonah 1:2. But Jonah would have been keenly aware of that trait already, for the Israelites had suffered greatly under the fierce aggression of this Assyrian tribe. Known for their evil and violence, the Ninevites must have been anathema to Jonah. How would we feel today if we were asked to preach to the masterminds of the September 11 attack? Would we want to see them receive forgiveness rather than punishment? Maybe we can at least understand Jonah's reticence when we view his situation from that perspective.

It's not surprising, then, that Jonah boarded a ship going in the exact opposite direction of Nineveh. But God wasn't about to let his wayward child get too far before he reminded Jonah who was in charge. "The LORD sent a great wind on the sea" (1:4), a wind that quickly produced a violent storm of a magnitude that could potentially sink the ship. Each of the sailors "cried out to his own god" (1:5), and they even threw the cargo into the sea, all in a frantic attempt to calm the storm. But neither gods nor lightening the ship's hold would bring an end to this storm. There was a disobedient child aboard, and God was determined to get his attention.

FIRST LOOKS

1. We're told in 1:3 that Jonah "ran away from the LORD." What's the difference between merely running away and running *away from* the Lord? What might this tell us about Jonah's character and beliefs?

2. Where was Jonah when the storm intensified, the sailors called out to their gods, and the cargo was thrown off the ship? Why do you think he was there?

⚡ 3. When the sailors cast lots to find out who was "responsible for this calamity" (1:7), they determined that it was Jonah. How did Jonah respond to their questions? When the sailors later asked Jonah what would calm the sea, what was his answer? How does this contrast with his earlier actions?

Read Jonah 1–2 again.

A WHALE OF A FISH

The scene on this ship at sea was chaotic. It's incredibly ironic that a man who had at first run from God's direct command would now: (1) acknowledge that the Lord created everything, (2) admit that he was to blame for the raging storm, and (3) instruct the sailors to toss him into the sea so they would be saved. How could a man who thought he could flee from God's presence later announce that the Lord had made the sea and land? How could he try to hide from the consequences of his actions and yet admit his responsibility? And how could Jonah unselfishly volunteer to be thrown in the sea to save these sailors when it was his disregard for others' lives that got him into this mess in the first place?

Also, in contrast to Jonah's sinful disobedience, his shipmates—who were obviously pagans since they worshiped a multitude of gods (1:5)—acted more "righteously" than Jonah. These sailors exhausted all other means before they relented and threw Jonah into the turbulent waves. We're again astounded at their compassion and sincere efforts to do what's right when they cried out, "Do not hold us accountable for killing an innocent man, for you, O LORD, have done as you pleased" (1:14) and later when they "offered a sacrifice to the LORD and made vows to him" (1:16) after the sea calmed down. Could it be that, even in the midst of this frantic and tumultuous situation, God was showing Jonah—and us as well—that he was ever mindful of the Gentiles' need for salvation?

But the story certainly didn't end there, for Jonah's adventure had only just begun. After being thrown overboard, our hapless hero was swallowed by a great fish. The text tells us the fish was *provided by the Lord,* a significant detail that emphasizes Who was actually orchestrating this journey. Jonah thought he was directing his own path—choosing to run and then encouraging the sailors to throw him overboard. But it's apparent that not only was God intent upon accomplishing his will, he would also ordain the means to get there.

We can't imagine what it was like to be swallowed by a whale, but Jonah must have felt sheer terror. However, he praised God by admitting, "You brought my life up from the pit" (2:6). And could it be that since Jonah had nowhere else to turn (in the belly of a whale that's especially true!), he turned to God in desperation, crying out, "What I have vowed I will make good"? (2:9) A chastised and repentant Jonah was now ready to travel in the direction God had commanded.

The fish burped, Jonah miraculously found himself on dry land, and a merciful God gave him a second chance: "Go to the great city of Nineveh and proclaim to it the message I give you" (3:1). Finally, Jonah was ready to proceed. With the best of intentions, God's prophet headed off, this time in the right direction. Until he met the hated Ninevites face to face, and his resolve crumbled.

TAKING IT IN

4. List several examples of how God subtly proved that *he* was directing Jonah's adventure. In light of all the ways God could

have forced Jonah to go to Nineveh, why do you think he
instead used such means as the sea and sailors to get Jonah's
attention and nudge him toward his calling?

5. Jonah's prayer in chapter 2 was written sometime *after* his experience—in hindsight. We could think of it this way: Jonah
reflected on the time when he was in the fish by beginning in
verse 1, "From inside the fish [I] prayed to the LORD [my]
God." He then continued with his memories of that time in
prayer, placing all of his actions in past tense. For example,
Jonah didn't ask to be saved; he thanked God for already doing
so. As Jonah looked back on this near-death experience, how
might that have changed his perceptions of the event?

Read Jonah 3–4 again.

A PETULANT PROPHET

Jonah began his walk through Nineveh, proclaiming that God intended to destroy the Ninevites if they didn't repent. We learn later in chapter 4 that Jonah still wanted them to suffer calamity, so imagine with us the tone of his voice and the vehemence of his gestures as he preached. We envision Jonah blasting the Ninevites with fiery words and haughty judgment gestured with a pointed finger. Maybe Jonah was even enjoying himself at this point!

Then, to Jonah's great dismay, we're told that the people "believed God" (3:5). They heeded Jonah's warning and took action, exhibiting that era's customs of repentance by fasting and covering themselves in sackcloth. The king and his nobles responded also, urging everyone to "call urgently on God" and "give up their evil ways" (3:8).

We have no idea if the Ninevites' repentance meant a lasting change, but it brought about the desired result: "[God] had compassion and did not bring upon them the destruction he had threatened" (3:10). Rather than being pleased for the people, however, Jonah was incensed. Isn't it interesting to note again the contrast between a "spiritual" prophet who reluctantly obeyed with a disobedient attitude—and a sinful people who simply believed God and then obeyed with repentant actions?

At this point, Jonah was *miserable*. Firmly believing that the Ninevites deserved dire punishment for their evil ways, he could focus on only one issue: his anger about the unfairness of God's love, grace, and forgiveness. Petulant, pouting, and deciding that he was fully righteous in his anger toward God, Jonah complained to God about his compassion. Didn't Jonah realize that he also needed and benefited from God's attributes of being "slow to anger and abounding in love" (4:2)? Jonah had experienced God's patience and love when he ran away from the Lord, and yet he complained that he was a "God who relents from sending calamity" (4:2). How could Jonah have so quickly forgotten the adventure with the whale and God's provision and protection?

God's response to Jonah's complaints was yet another rhetorical question, a piercing one. "Have you any right to be angry?" God asked (4:4). First, we should note that Jonah's anger was not like the instant anger we feel from an emotional or physical injury. God's query calls into account Jonah's motives, his attitudes of self-righteousness and judgment, and his decision to set himself up as "judge." Jonah actually placed himself at the apex, granting himself the right to judge not only the Ninevites, but God as well.

We may wonder how this man, reluctant prophet and defiant servant, dared to judge God. But before we (ironically) set up ourselves to condemn Jonah, we must realize that the question, "Have you any right to be angry?" speaks to our hearts too. How many times have we dared to put ourselves in the same position as Jonah—as judge and jury of God himself? Like Jonah's, our judgments are couched in complaining and self-pity, with a hint of self-righteousness thrown in. "How can you be a fair God and allow my divorce?" we ask. "How can you be a loving God and permit poverty? If you're a God of peace, why do you tolerate war?" Aren't we demanding that God answer to us when we ask those types of questions?

Rather than responding to Jonah's complaints with much-deserved anger, however, God patiently gave Jonah an object lesson. As God's prophet sat in the shade of a shelter and continued to pout—watching the city of Nineveh and evidently still hoping God would send destruction—the Lord made a vine grow. Maybe the shelter's shade decreased as the day wore on, for Jonah obviously relished and needed the vine's protection from the hot sun. We're specifically told that "God provided a vine" (4:6), but we have no indication that Jonah acknowledged the gift—or thanked God for it.

However, God wasn't finished with his lesson. The very next morning the Lord created a worm that chewed on the vine until it withered and died. To drive home his point, God then sent a "scorching east wind, and the sun blazed on Jonah's head so that he grew faint...[and] wanted to die" (4:8). When Jonah insisted, "It would be better for me to die" (4:8), God responded again with nearly the same rhetorical question as before: "Do you have a right to be angry about the vine?" (4:9).

Always a wise and loving teacher, God used his creation as a visual aid to illustrate Jonah's false reasoning, selfishness, and lack of compassion. The Lord pointed out that, though Jonah had no influence on whether the vine lived or died, he showed more compassion for a mere plant than he did for the people of Nineveh. And as the sovereign God also clearly emphasized, he would continue to reach out to *all* peoples, even the pagan Gentiles.

God's last question of Jonah—"Should I not be concerned about that great city?" (4:11)—demands that Jonah answer the true Judge of the world. *Which is more important?* he asks. *A vine? Or people? Your self-seeking desires? Or my love and compassion for needy souls?* Today, as people still in desperate need of his grace, mercy, and love, we'd best be ready to answer his question.

Making It Real

6. Describe a time, if any, when you set yourself up as a judgmental god, pronouncing a sentence upon someone (or possibly an organization or a people) in need of salvation. Whom have you labeled "beyond redemption"? Does anyone ever reach that point? Explain.

7. Because Jonah's prayer in chapter 2 was written in past tense, we know it is reflective. Do you think our perspective changes when we can look back on a past experience in its entirety? If so, why?

8. How has an unforgiving attitude kept you from talking about your faith with someone? What steps can you take to change that?

9. God is a God of both mercy and justice. Those two traits may seem to be a contradiction, but we as human beings can also be both merciful and just. Can you think of a time when you

exhibited both of these qualities when dealing with someone?
with a son or daughter? a child you teach? a subordinate at
work? Describe the situation.

10. Can you think of a person who has wounded you or someone
you love so deeply that you've held on to your hurt and anger,
telling yourself that your pain is justified? If you told God about
your anger like Jonah did, how do you think he might respond?
What steps can you take to forgive this person as God does?

LEADER'S NOTES

STUDY 1: "WHERE ARE YOU?"

Question 2. The consequences of the curse for Adam and Eve included what was evidently nonexistent before they sinned: *pain.* Eve (and therefore all women) would now feel pain in childbirth (Genesis 3:16). And though God earlier referred to Adam's tending the garden as "work" (2:15), it must have been far from physically demanding since it's now described as "painful toil" (3:17).

Question 7. Satan began a pattern of intimating that *God is at fault; he's denying you!* when he asked, "Did God really say, 'You must not eat from any tree in the garden'?" (Genesis 3:1). Satan knew very well that was not what God said! But Eve fell for the bait of blaming and misrepresenting God when, adding to God's command, she replied, "and you must not touch it" (3:3).

STUDY 2: "IS ANYTHING TOO HARD FOR THE LORD?"

Question 3. When God reveals himself to humans in visible form, it is called a *theophany.* He has revealed himself in various ways throughout history. God appeared as a smoking firepot with a blazing torch when he ratified his covenant with Abram (Genesis 15:17), and many years later he appeared to Moses as a burning bush (Exodus 3:2). When Moses led the Israelites to the Promised Land, God was a pillar of cloud and a pillar of fire to guide them by day and night (Exodus 13:21). And Jesus Christ is both the Son of God and Visible God at the same time!

Question 5. Sometimes we misinterpret God's promises to mean that we will never suffer. Matthew 6:25-33 speaks of God's provision that "all these things [food, drink, and clothing] will be given to you." However, Paul painted a realistic picture in Acts 14:22: "We must go through many hardships to enter the kingdom of God." God will indeed provide for us, but we dare not assume this means a life of ease.

STUDY 3: "WHAT IS YOUR NAME?"

Question 2. In Genesis 28:17, after Jacob's famous dream of the angels ascending and descending a ladder to heaven, he declared, "This is none other than the house of God; this is the gate of heaven." Later, when the angels of God met him at Mahanaim, Jacob proclaimed, "This is the camp of God!" (32:2). The parallels couldn't have been lost on Jacob: God sent angels to visit him when he left his own land and then once again when he returned.

Question 9. We're told that Jacob struggled *all night* with the Man (32:24). Jacob's persistence (not giving in until he was supernaturally crippled and even then, still clinging to the Man, demanding a blessing) was evidently significant to the Israelites: Verse 32 tells us that they never again ate the "tendon attached to the socket of the hip." By observing this dietary restriction, they would forever remember Jacob's face-to-face encounter with God.

STUDY 4: "WHAT IS THAT IN YOUR HAND?"

Question 5. The Israelites were in awe of the "I AM" name of God, which may be a play on words for *Lord,* or *Yahweh.* Therefore, it's no surprise that when Jesus said, "Before Abraham was born, I am!" the Jews attempted to stone him (John 8:58-59). Later, just before his crucifixion when the soldiers came to arrest him, Jesus identified himself by saying, "I am he." In response to the awesome power of the Name, the soldiers all "drew back and *fell to the ground*" (John 18:5-6, emphasis added).

Question 6. The cobra was such a significant animal to the Egyptians that the pharaohs wore a metal cobra as a king's crown. We don't know if this pharaoh wore one, but we do know that God used Aaron's staff to prove God's supreme power as the King: Aaron's snake ate the two snakes that the pharaoh's sorcerers produced (Exodus 7:12).

STUDY 5: "WHY HAVE YOU BEATEN YOUR DONKEY?"

Question 1. It's easy to condemn Balaam for his conflicting responses of believing God yet disobeying him. But so often we respond the same way: Even though we believe and trust in God, we doubt and disobey him. We have plenty of examples of this in Scripture, too: the questioning father of the boy with an evil spirit (Mark 9:24); the disciples' petty arguments about their importance (Luke 22:24); and Peter's denials of Jesus (Matthew 26:69-75), to name just a few.

Question 6. The use of the word *revealed* in the New Testament is interesting to study. We might read Romans 8:18 and assume that the "glory that will be revealed" means it will suddenly come into sight from somewhere else. Isn't that what a revelation is? Actually, the revelation of the glory means that *it was there all along;* we just didn't *see* it with our eyes! You might want to check Romans 16:25-27 and 1 Peter 1:3-5 for other "revelations."

STUDY 6: "WHAT ARE YOU DOING DOWN ON YOUR FACE?"

Question 5. Wherever the Israelites went—and whether they won or lost a battle—they represented the one true God. Therefore, a loss would be interpreted by the victors (pagans who worshiped many gods) as a sign that *their* gods were more powerful than the Israelites' God. No wonder Joshua was so concerned about God's reputation!

In the New Testament, we find a parallel situation: Acts 11:26 says "the disciples were called Christians first at Antioch," for they represented Christ. Because of severe persecution—to the extent that Stephen was stoned to death—the believing Jews in Jerusalem were scattered. Some of them went to Antioch, and as they continued "telling them the good news" (Acts 11:20), Jews *and* Gentiles were saved. But it wasn't long before the newly named Christians in Antioch were also persecuted. Today, carrying Christ's name is a privilege—but one that can still bring pain.

Question 11. Certainly, the valley where Achan was killed would have been filled with sad associations for the Israelites: stealing, lies, sin, guilt, and death. But Hosea 2:15 presents a totally opposite view, for Hosea quoted the Lord's assertion that "I will make the Valley of Achor a door of hope." Once again we're reminded of God's grace, forgiveness, and love. This valley—a place of sin, sadness, and death—is transformed by God and given a new meaning: *hope!* When we repent, our "valleys of trouble" become "doors of hope."

STUDY 7: "AM I NOT SENDING YOU?"

Question 4. Gideon asked the Lord to stay until he brought him an "offering." It's no coincidence that the food and broth he offered to the Lord closely paralleled a priestly offering. Leviticus 9:24 says, "Fire came out from the presence of the LORD and consumed the burnt offering," and Hebrews 13:11-12 speaks of *the* High Priest's offering, Jesus Christ himself. In this passage in the book of Judges, the beautiful imagery of the Priest's accepting Gideon's offering becomes a worthy beginning to the Israelites' reconciliation with their God.

Question 5. For a good part of their conversation in chapter 6, Gideon didn't know who this visitor was. But once the Angel of the Lord touched the food offering with his staff and fire flared up, Gideon understood that this was none other than the Lord himself. At that point, Gideon exclaimed, "Ah, Sovereign LORD! I have seen the angel of the LORD face to face!" (Judges 6:22). It sounds as if he were merely excited, but the next comment by the Lord revealed what else Gideon was feeling: fear. Israelites believed that seeing God's face brought instant death, so Gideon—the "mighty warrior"—evidently cowered in fright, expecting to die. When the Lord responded with encouragement, it is no wonder Gideon built an altar there and named it "The LORD is Peace."

STUDY 8: "HAVE YOU ANY RIGHT TO BE ANGRY?"

Question 1. Jonah appeared to be quite the conflicted prophet. He blatantly defied God and yet, rather than being unable to sleep because of a guilty conscience, he slept soundly below deck—in a raging storm. When asked by the sailors, "From what people are you?" Jonah's response was yet another enigma: "I am a Hebrew and I worship the LORD" (Jonah 1:9). And in verse 10 we read: "They [the sailors] knew he was running away from the LORD, because *he had already told them so*" (emphasis added). Yet Jonah was no different from us—or other biblical characters. The father's cry in Mark 9:24 speaks for all of us: "I do believe; help me overcome my unbelief!"

Question 3. In the Old Testament and in the beginning of the New Testament, the Holy Spirit did not permanently dwell within God's people. Until the Holy Spirit came at Pentecost (Acts 2), believers needed another way to discern God's will. Therefore, many used the method of "casting lots," which could have meant casting stones or sticks into a container and drawing them out to reveal the answer. (We're not sure about the process, but it may have involved using black and white stones or even arrows.) God then "directed" the outcome. But it wasn't only God's people who cast lots. Pagans—like the sailors in this passage—would use this method to determine the will of their "gods" or, as evidenced here in the book of Jonah, to allow their gods to point to a specific person.

FOR FURTHER STUDY

If you enjoyed this Fisherman Resource, you might want to explore our full line of Fisherman Resources and Bible Studyguides. The following books offer time-tested Fisherman inductive Bible studies for individuals or groups.

FISHERMAN RESOURCES

The Art of Spiritual Listening: Responding to God's Voice Amid the Noise of Life by Alice Fryling

Balm in Gilead by Dudley Delffs

The Essential Bible Guide by Whitney T. Kuniholm

Questions from the God Who Needs No Answers: What Is He Really Asking of You? by Carolyn and Craig Williford

Reckless Faith: Living Passionately as Imperfect Christians by Jo Kadlecek

Soul Strength: Spiritual Courage for the Battles of Life by Pam Lau

FISHERMAN BIBLE STUDYGUIDES

Topical Studies

Angels by Vinita Hampton Wright

Becoming Women of Purpose by Ruth Haley Barton

Building Your House on the Lord: A Firm Foundation for Family Life (Revised Edition) by Steve and Dee Brestin

Discipleship: The Growing Christian's Lifestyle by James and Martha Reapsome

Doing Justice, Showing Mercy: Christian Action in Today's World by Vinita Hampton Wright

Encouraging Others: Biblical Models for Caring by Lin Johnson

The End Times: Discovering What the Bible Says by E. Michael Rusten

Examining the Claims of Jesus by Dee Brestin

Friendship: Portraits in God's Family Album by Steve and Dee Brestin

The Fruit of the Spirit: Growing in Christian Character by Stuart Briscoe

Great Doctrines of the Bible by Stephen Board

Great Passages of the Bible by Carol Plueddemann

Great Prayers of the Bible by Carol Plueddemann

Growing Through Life's Challenges by James and Martha Reapsome

Guidance & God's Will by Tom and Joan Stark

Heart Renewal: Finding Spiritual Refreshment by Ruth Goring

Higher Ground: Steps Toward Christian Maturity by Steve and Dee
Brestin

Images of Redemption: God's Unfolding Plan Through the Bible by Ruth
E. Van Reken

Integrity: Character from the Inside Out by Ted W. Engstrom and Robert
C. Larson

Lifestyle Priorities by John White

Marriage: Learning from Couples in Scripture by R. Paul and Gail Stevens

Miracles by Robbie Castleman

One Body, One Spirit: Building Relationships in the Church by Dale and
Sandy Larsen

The Parables of Jesus by Gladys Hunt

Parenting with Purpose and Grace by Alice Fryling

Prayer: Discovering What Scripture Says by Timothy Jones and Jill
Zook-Jones

The Prophets: God's Truth Tellers by Vinita Hampton Wright

Proverbs and Parables: God's Wisdom for Living by Dee Brestin

Satisfying Work: Christian Living from Nine to Five by R. Paul Stevens
and Gerry Schoberg

Senior Saints: Growing Older in God's Family by James and Martha Reapsome

The Sermon on the Mount: The God Who Understands Me by Gladys M. Hunt

Speaking Wisely: Exploring the Power of Words by Poppy Smith

Spiritual Disciplines: The Tasks of a Joyful Life by Larry Sibley

Spiritual Gifts by Karen Dockrey

Spiritual Hunger: Filling Your Deepest Longings by Jim and Carol Plueddemann

A Spiritual Legacy: Faith for the Next Generation by Chuck and Winnie Christensen

Spiritual Warfare by A. Scott Moreau

The Ten Commandments: God's Rules for Living by Stuart Briscoe

Ultimate Hope for Changing Times by Dale and Sandy Larsen

When Faith Is All You Have: A Study of Hebrews 11 by Ruth E. Van Reken

Where Your Treasure Is: What the Bible Says About Money by James and Martha Reapsome

Who Is God? by David P. Seemuth

Who Is Jesus? In His Own Words by Ruth E. Van Reken

Who Is the Holy Spirit? by Barbara H. Knuckles and Ruth E. Van Reken

Wisdom for Today's Woman: Insights from Esther by Poppy Smith

Witnesses to All the World: God's Heart for the Nations by Jim and Carol Plueddemann

Women at Midlife: Embracing the Challenges by Jeanie Miley

Worship: Discovering What Scripture Says by Larry Sibley

Bible Book Studies

Genesis: Walking with God by Margaret Fromer and Sharrel Keyes

Exodus: God Our Deliverer by Dale and Sandy Larsen

Ruth: Relationships That Bring Life by Ruth Haley Barton
Ezra and Nehemiah: A Time to Rebuild by James Reapsome
(For Esther, see Topical Studies, *Wisdom for Today's Woman*)
Job: Trusting Through Trials by Ron Klug
Psalms: A Guide to Prayer and Praise by Ron Klug
Proverbs: Wisdom That Works by Vinita Hampton Wright
Ecclesiastes: A Time for Everything by Stephen Board
Song of Songs: A Dialogue of Intimacy by James Reapsome
Jeremiah: The Man and His Message by James Reapsome
Jonah, Habakkuk, and Malachi: Living Responsibly by Margaret Fromer
    and Sharrel Keyes
Matthew: People of the Kingdom by Larry Sibley
Mark: God in Action by Chuck and Winnie Christensen
Luke: Following Jesus by Sharrel Keyes
John: The Living Word by Whitney Kuniholm
Acts 1–12: God Moves in the Early Church by Chuck and Winnie
    Christensen
Acts 13–28, see *Paul* under Character Studies
Romans: The Christian Story by James Reapsome
1 Corinthians: Problems and Solutions in a Growing Church by Charles
    and Ann Hummel
Strengthened to Serve: 2 Corinthians by Jim and Carol Plueddemann
Galatians, Titus, and Philemon: Freedom in Christ by Whitney Kuniholm
Ephesians: Living in God's Household by Robert Baylis
Philippians: God's Guide to Joy by Ron Klug
Colossians: Focus on Christ by Luci Shaw
Letters to the Thessalonians by Margaret Fromer and Sharrel Keyes
Letters to Timothy: Discipleship in Action by Margaret Fromer and
    Sharrel Keyes
Hebrews: Foundations for Faith by Gladys Hunt
James: Faith in Action by Chuck and Winnie Christensen

1 and 2 Peter, Jude: Called for a Purpose by Steve and Dee Brestin
1, 2, 3 John: How Should a Christian Live? by Dee Brestin
Revelation. The Lamb Who Is the Lion by Gladys Hunt

Bible Character Studies

Abraham: Model of Faith by James Reapsome
David: Man After God's Own Heart by Robbie Castleman
Elijah: Obedience in a Threatening World by Robbie Castleman
Great People of the Bible by Carol Plueddemann
King David: Trusting God for a Lifetime by Robbie Castleman
Men Like Us: Ordinary Men, Extraordinary God by Paul Heidebrecht
    and Ted Scheuermann
Moses: Encountering God by Greg Asimakoupoulos
Paul: Thirteenth Apostle (Acts 13–28) by Chuck and Winnie Christensen
Women Like Us: Wisdom for Today's Issues by Ruth Haley Barton
Women Who Achieved for God by Winnie Christensen
Women Who Believed God by Winnie Christensen

ABOUT THE AUTHORS

Craig Williford, president of Denver Seminary, and Carolyn Williford, an author and conference speaker, both have a deep appreciation for God's Word and how it can convict, teach, refine, and bless. The Willifords are professionally trained Christian educators with a high regard for biblical study that is theologically, contextually, and hermeneutically correct, yet is also interesting and creative and actively engages the student in its content. With over twenty years in pastoral ministry, Craig and Carolyn also share a deep desire to minister to the *person* who will be reading and studying these passages. The Willifords have two sons, both married, and a black Labrador named Wendy.

Printed in the United States
by Baker & Taylor Publisher Services